Pocket GCSE Latin Etymological Lexicon

ALSO AVAILABLE FROM BLOOMSBURY

Pocket GCSE Latin Etymological Lexicon

BLOOMSBURY ACADEMIC
LONDON · NEW YORK · OXFORD · NEW DELHI · SYDNEY

BLOOMSBURY ACADEMIC
Bloomsbury Publishing Plc
50 Bedford Square, London, WC1B 3DP, UK
1385 Broadway, New York, NY 10018, USA
29 Earlsfort Terrace, Dublin 2, Ireland

BLOOMSBURY, BLOOMSBURY ACADEMIC and the Diana logo are trademarks of
Bloomsbury Publishing Plc

First published in Great Britain 2022

Cover design: Terry Woodley
Cover image © Ancient Rome *forum Romanum*. Illustration from 19th century.
clu/Getty.

A catalogue record for this book is available from the British Library.

Library of Congress Cataloging-in-Publication Data

Names: Mackenzie, Caroline K., author.
Title: Pocket GCSE Latin etymological lexicon / Caroline K. Mackenzie.
Description: New York : Bloomsbury Academic, 2022.
Identifiers: LCCN 2022008909 | ISBN 9781350320758 (paperback) |
ISBN 9781350320772 (ebook) | ISBN 9781350320765 (epub) | ISBN 9781350320789
Subjects: LCSH: Latin language–Etymology–Dictionaries–English. |
LCGFT: Dictionaries.
Classification: LCC PA2342 .M26 2022 | DDC 472/.03—dc23/eng/20220302
LC record available at https://lccn.loc.gov/2022008909

ISBN: PB: 978-1-3503-2075-8
          ePDF: 978-1-3503-2077-2
          eBook: 978-1-3503-2076-5

Typeset by RefineCatch Limited, Bungay, Suffolk
To find out more about our authors and books visit www.bloomsbury.com
and sign up for our newsletters.

For my parents, with love and thanks.

Preface

The idea for this book arose from many happy hours spent with my pupils who were striving to learn their Latin vocabulary. Together we devised a game where we would think of an English derivative from a Latin word, which would then provide a clue to the meaning of the Latin; e.g. *rideo* means 'I laugh' or 'I smile', and some English derivatives are 'deride' or 'ridiculous'. We soon discovered that the Latin words were easy to recall and learning became much more efficient as well as fun.

Around this time, I used to hear commuters on the train mumbling to themselves as they sought the answers to their daily crossword. Often, I realised that Latin words were behind both the clues and the answers. It seemed the above technique of associating derivatives with their Latin origin might help with word puzzles and similar activities, too.

The purpose of this book is threefold. First, it includes all the words on the respective Defined Vocabulary Lists for both the Oxford Cambridge and RSA ('the OCR') Latin GCSE syllabus and the WJEC Eduqas ('the Eduqas') Latin GCSE syllabus. Therefore, the book can be used as a revision aid for GCSE pupils studying for either of these qualifications. Secondly, the book is intended as a secret weapon for anyone tackling crosswords or word games, where the associations between Latin vocabulary and the English derivatives will spark the imagination and encourage a deluge of possible answers. Last and certainly not least, the overriding aim of this book is to provide enjoyment. I hope you will find it fun, challenging and a fitting celebration of the magnificent Latin language.

The original edition of this book, 'A Latin Lexicon: an Illustrated Compendium of Latin words and English derivatives' was published by Archaeopress in 2020 and is available as a full colour hardback.

Introduction

Layout of the book – main entries, appendices and key to asterisks

There are 413 main entries in total, representing words from each of the OCR Latin GCSE Defined Vocabulary List ('the OCR List') and the Eduqas Latin GCSE Defined Vocabulary List ('the Eduqas List'). Most of the words appear on both the OCR List and the Eduqas List and it should be assumed that this is the case unless an entry has been asterisked. A single asterisk (*) indicates that the entry appears on the Eduqas List alone. Two asterisks (**) indicate that the entry appears on both lists but it is slightly different on each and an explanatory footnote has been added accordingly. Three asterisks (***) indicate that the entry appears on the OCR List alone.

The Eduqas List has 440 entries in total – 355 of these are in the main entries. The remaining 85 words on the Eduqas List do not lend themselves to derivatives and have therefore been included separately, by simple list, in Appendix One where you will also find some more information about the Eduqas List.

The OCR List has 450 entries in total – 364 of these are in the main entries. In addition, the main entries include 10 irregular comparative and superlative forms of adjectives which are part of the OCR specification, and all the prescribed cardinal numbers (1 to 10, 100 and 1,000). The remaining 86 words on the OCR List do not lend themselves to derivatives and have therefore been included separately, by simple list, in Appendix Two where you will also find some more information about the OCR List.

Whichever GCSE syllabus you are following, if you learn all the vocabulary by heart, you will be able to tackle translations and comprehensions with confidence and flair. Words in the vocabulary list are quite simply the building blocks that you need to achieve a solid standing in Latin. Combined with a firm grasp of the grammar, knowledge of the vocabulary really is the key to success.

The following paragraphs explain the information which is included in the main entries. As mentioned above, the appendices are presented as simple lists, with relevant grammatical information for each entry but no derivatives.

Nouns

Nouns are shown in the nominative singular then the genitive singular. The genitive provides the stem. The gender is also given: masculine (masc.), feminine (fem.) or neuter (neut.). Underneath each noun, the declension (or group) to which that noun belongs is shown as 1st, 2nd, 3rd, 4th or 5th. The numbers are presented in this way to distinguish them from the numbers of conjugations (shown as first, second, etc.) which apply to the verbs.

Adjectives

Adjectives are shown in the following order: masculine, feminine, then neuter. If the feminine is the same as the masculine, it is not repeated so the two forms shown are: masculine/feminine, then neuter. Some 3rd declension adjectives are given instead with the genitive singular as this provides the stem, e.g. 'felix, (gen.) felicis'.[1]

Verbs

Verbs are shown with their principal parts, which give the following information: present tense (first person singular), present infinitive (which indicates to which conjugation the verb belongs), perfect tense (first person singular) and, where applicable, perfect passive participle. The fourth principal part of a verb is often the best place to start when trying to guess a derivative from that verb.

Verbs belong to different conjugations, or families, which determine how they are formed. The conjugations are shown beneath the principal parts as first, second, third or fourth. The numbers are presented in this way to distinguish them from the

---

[1] On these types of adjectives see Taylor p. 26.

numbers of declensions (shown as 1st, 2nd, etc.) which apply to the nouns. Some verbs are 'mixed' conjugations and are shown as third/fourth. These verbs are treated as third conjugation because their infinitive ends in *-ere* but their present, imperfect and future tenses are the same as the fourth conjugation.[2]

Deponent verbs are marked as such. These are verbs which are passive in form but active in meaning. There are also three semi-deponent verbs (but these are only on the OCR List).[3]

Adverbs

The adverbs included are indeclinable which means they do not change their endings.

Cases

A case, such as the ablative or dative, is used for a noun, pronoun or adjective to show the role it is playing in the sentence. The prepositions included in this book are shown with the case by which they are usually followed e.g. 'ad (+ accusative)' (to, towards) and it is worth learning both parts together. Most verbs are followed by an accusative and this is the default unless the entry states otherwise. However, some verbs use the dative e.g. 'credo' (I trust) (literally, 'I give my trust *to* you'). These verbs are

---

[2] On mixed conjugations see Taylor p. 68.

[3] On deponent and semi-deponent verbs see Taylor pp. 99-101.

shown as taking the dative as, again, it is worth learning this at the same time as the meaning of the verb.

The names of the different cases are themselves Latin derivatives and these may help explain the purpose of each case:

'nominative' from 'nomen' (name) It 'names' the subject of a sentence or clause.	Subject
'vocative' from 'voco' (I call) Used for addressing or 'calling' someone.	Addressing
'accusative' from 'accuso'[4] (I accuse) It aims at or 'holds accountable' the object of a sentence or clause.	Object
'genitive' from 'gens' (family, people) It denotes that something belongs to another, or is 'of' another (as if of its 'family').	Of
'dative' from 'do' (I give) ('do, dare, dedi, *datus*') Usually denotes giving: 'I give a gift *to* you' or, 'this gift is *for* you'.	To, for
'ablative' from 'a, ab' (from, by) and 'ablatus' (see 'aufero, auferre, abstuli, *ablatus*') (carry away) Indicates 'away from', or simply 'from', 'by', or sometimes 'with'.	From, by, with

---

[4] 'accuso' is not on either the Eduqas List or the OCR List. It means 'I accuse, blame, or find fault with' and the connection here seems to be that the accusative case 'aims at', 'focuses on' or 'holds accountable' the object of a sentence or clause.

'Irregular' words

Some Latin words do not belong to one of the standard declensions or conjugations. They are known as 'irregular' and are shown throughout this book as 'irreg.'

Choice of derivatives

This is by no means an exhaustive list of all the possible derivatives. Many of the Latin words have numerous derivatives in English but I have tried to limit the number of derivatives per word to a maximum of six, except where there is a cross-reference to another entry where one or two additional ones may be included. There is also space on each page for you to add some more derivatives if you wish to do so.

Cross-references are marked up 'cf.' followed by the relevant Latin word, being the first word in the respective entry. If the cross-reference applies to the whole entry, I have included it on a separate line from the derivatives. If the cross-reference applies to one or more specific derivatives, then I have included it immediately following that derivative (or those derivatives) and not on a separate line.

If a derivative can be used in the English language in both its singular and plural forms (e.g. 'curator' and 'curators') I have simply included one of these (usually the singular). However, where a derivative gives us, say, both a verb and a noun, or both an adjective and an adverb, I have often included both, despite their apparent similarity. This is not repetition for its own sake but to demonstrate how ubiquitous the derivatives are in our language. Also, some students may be familiar with one derivative but not the others and, from a didactic point of view, my aim is to facilitate the learning of the Latin word by association with an already familiar English word.

I have not attempted to explain or distinguish whether derivatives come from the Latin verb or noun as that is beyond the scope of this book. Sometimes a Latin noun and verb (e.g. 'imperator' and 'impero') give us derivatives (empire, imperious, etc.) that can usefully be associated with both the noun and verb for the purposes of learning vocabulary. If the number of derivatives allows, I have included different ones for, say, the noun and the verb and cross-referenced them.

Some derivatives may seem obvious, e.g. 'resist' from 'resisto' whereas others are more surprising e.g. why does a 'tandem' bike derive from 'tandem' (at last)? If we translate 'tandem' as 'at length' this begins to make more sense when we think of a tandem bike (for two people) simply as a lengthened version of a one-person bike. 'Tandem' is often confused with 'tamen' (however) but by imagining a picture of a tandem bike (see page 120) and knowing the pun in the meaning, the distinction between the two words can easily be made.

For consistency, words that can end in either '-ise' or '-ize' are shown throughout with the ending '-ise'.

The derivatives are listed in alphabetical order within each entry for ease of reference.

Latin words and phrases in common usage

Some words and phrases which we use in English are taken direct from the Latin (e.g. 'alter ego'). One could argue that these are not strictly 'derivatives', and that they are simply Latin. I have, however, included them where I believe they are in sufficiently common usage to be familiar to many, if not all, readers. They are shown in inverted commas, e.g. 'bona fide'. For their meanings, please see the Glossary.

Derivatives in other languages

Of course, there are many Latin derivatives in other European languages such as Italian and French. With a few exceptions, limitations of space have precluded me from including other languages but this can be a very useful way for students to learn their vocabulary and there is space on each page for such comparisons to be noted. A good knowledge of Latin can improve one's vocabulary not only in English but in many other modern languages.

'Double derivatives'

The number of cross-references ('double derivatives' if you will) is large and while I have included most of them, for reasons of space and not wishing to clutter the pages, I have left some of these for you to spot for yourself. For example, 'facio' (I make) appears in many compound verbs and their derivatives (in forms such as '-fact', '-fic' and '-fy'). Likewise, prefixes such as 'pro-' (in front of) and 're-' (...back) recur frequently.

Names

Names, e.g. Benedict (see 'bene' and 'dico'), can be identified as such since they are the only derivatives that are given with an initial capital letter. There are numerous brand names (clothing lines, food products, furniture shops, etc.) which make good use of Latin (and Greek) derivatives. For copyright reasons I have not included them in the book, but readers may naturally be reminded of some of these when studying the meanings of the Latin words and it can be a useful way for students to remember vocabulary.

'It's all Greek . . .'

Of course, many Latin words themselves derive from Ancient Greek, e.g. 'hora' from 'ὥρα' (transliterated 'hora') but I have not attempted to show these as the aim of this book is to connect the Latin words to English. Ancient Greek is a wonderful language and deserves a derivatives book of its own.

Genders

Some Latin nouns have very similar masculine and feminine forms (e.g. 'deus' for god and 'dea' for goddess) and for completeness I have included both in the main entries where applicable.

Months of the year

The original Roman calendar comprised a ten-month year. Of those ten months, September was the seventh month, October was the eighth, November was the ninth, and December was the tenth. This explains why these months' names derive from their respective numbers. The additional two months (which make up our twelve) also have a Roman association – July after the dictator Gaius Julius Caesar (who was born in that month) and August after his adopted son and heir, the emperor Augustus.

Themes

I have avoided including terms which are very specialist e.g. legal phrases such as 'res ipsa loquitur' (the thing speaks for itself) although another legal term 'caveat emptor' (buyer beware) may be more familiar from its use in our conveyancing system and therefore is included. Musical terms such as 'cadence' from 'cado' (I fall) will be well-known to musicians but have only been included if I believe they may also be familiar to other readers, too. Even the world of information technology embraces Latin derivatives such as 'cursor' from 'curro' (I run) and 'delete' from 'deleo' (I destroy). While 'dormy' from 'dormio' (I sleep) is probably only known to golfers and was a new discovery for me, I could not resist including it.[5]

Other themes that I frequently encountered in my research (perhaps unsurprisingly) were those of flowers ('gladiolus') and nature ('brevipennate'), the church ('Advent' and 'laetare'), medicine and anatomy ('vertebra'), vocations ('horologist'), sport ('equestrian') and theatre (stage directions given in Latin such as 'loquitur', 'exeunt', etc.). You may wish to use this book as the starting point for collecting further derivatives within a theme of your choice.

Derivatives in grammar

Even the word 'derivative' is itself a derivative, being literally something flowing downstream (the verb 'derivare' means to turn into another channel or to divert from). Likewise, 'declension' derives from 'declinare' (to bend away from), 'conjugation' from 'coniugare' (to join together or to connect) and 'language' from

---

[5] It means a player is as many holes ahead as there are still to play so (s)he cannot lose even if (s)he goes to sleep.

'lingua' (tongue). Many other grammatical terms appear throughout the derivatives given in this book as summarised below. (For the derivation of the names of cases, see 'Cases' above.)

'active' from 'ago' (I do, act)

'adjective' from 'ad' (to, towards) and 'iacio' (I throw)

'adverb' from 'ad' (to, towards) and 'verbum' (word)

'case' from 'cado' (I fall)

'dictionary' from 'dico' (I say)

'feminine' from 'femina' (woman)

'imperative' from 'impero' (I order)

'noun' from 'nomen' (name)

'object' from 'iacio' (I throw)

'passive' from 'patior' (I suffer, endure)

'preposition' from 'pono' (I place, put)

'sentence' from 'sentio' (I feel)

'subject' from 'sub' (under) and 'iacio' (I throw)

'tense' from 'tempus' (time)

'verb' from 'verbum' (word)

'vocabulary' from 'voco' (I call)

Further reading

For more detailed etymology and the meanings of any of the words in this book, see *The Chambers Dictionary* (Revised Thirteenth Edition, Chambers Harrap Publishers Ltd., 2016).

As a guide to the grammar, I strongly recommend John Taylor's *Essential GCSE Latin* (Third Edition, Bloomsbury, 2017) which sets out the rules succinctly and includes excellent practice passages.

For details of the specifications for the OCR (Oxford Cambridge and RSA) examination board's qualification in GCSE Latin, including the full Defined Vocabulary List, see: https://www.ocr.org.uk/qualifications/gcse/latin-j282-from-2016/

For details of the specifications for the WJEC Eduqas examination board's qualification in GCSE Latin, including the full Defined Vocabulary List, see: https://www.eduqas.co.uk/qualifications/latin-gcse/

Latin phrases and their abbreviations

It would be remiss not to showcase throughout this book some of the common Latin phrases and their abbreviations that we use. For completeness, I set them out here with a literal translation for each. (They also appear in the Glossary.)

cf.   'confer' (compare)

e.g.   'exempli gratia' (for the sake of example)

etc.   'et cetera' (and the others)

N.B.   'nota bene' (note well)

vide   (see)

Other abbreviations used in this book

fem. feminine

gen. genitive

indecl. indeclinable (does not change its endings)

irreg. irregular

masc. masculine

neut. neuter

pl. plural

Glossary: Latin words and phrases in common usage

adsum	*I am present; I am here*
alma mater	*one's former university, school or college (literally, 'nourishing mother')*
alter ego	*one's second self*
ante meridiem or a.m.	*before midday; morning*
anno domini or A.D.	*in the year of our Lord*
bona fide	*in good faith; genuine*
carpe diem	*seize the day*
caveat emptor	*let the buyer beware; it is the buyer's responsibility*
ceteris paribus or cet. par.	*other things being equal*

confer or **cf.**	*compare*
curriculum vitae or **C.V.**	*a summary of one's life, especially details of education and career (literally, 'the course of life')*
et alia or **et al.**	*and other things*
et cetera or **etc.**	*and the rest; and so on*
exeat	*formal leave of absence (literally, 'let him or her go out')*
exempli gratia or **e.g.**	*for (the sake of) example*
homo sapiens	*the human species (literally, 'wise human')*
ibidem or **ib.** or **ibid.**	*in the same place (used when referring to a book, article, etc. already cited in a directly preceding note or reference)*
idem or **id.**	*the same; as mentioned before*
id est or **i.e.**	*that is*
inter alia	*among other things*
inter nos	*between ourselves*
ipso facto	*by that very fact*
mea culpa	*(by) my fault*
modus operandi	*a way of working; mode of operation*
nota bene or **N. B.**	*note well; take note*
per annum or **p.a.**	*each year*

per capita	*counting by heads; for each person*
per centum **or *per cent.***	*for each hundred; percentage*
post meridiem **or *p.m.***	*after midday; afternoon*
post scriptum **or *P.S.***	*an addition to the completed text of a book; introduces addition to a letter or other message (literally, 'written after')*
prima facie	*on first appearance; at first sight*
pro rata	*in proportion*
pros and cons	*advantages and disadvantages (from 'pro' and 'contra' so literally, 'for and against')*
pro tempore **or *pro tem.***	*for the time being*
quidnunc	*an inquisitive, gossiping person (literally, 'what now?')*
quid pro quo	*something given or taken as equivalent to another (literally, 'something for something')*
quod erat demonstrandum **or *Q.E.D.***	*which was to be demonstrated or proved*
quod vide **or *q.v.***	*which see; see the thing just mentioned*
re	*concerning; with reference to (literally, '[in] the matter')*
semper fidelis	*always faithful*
semper idem	*always the same*
semper paratus	*always ready*
sic	*so; thus (often shown within brackets in quoted text to indicate that the original source is being strictly reproduced even though it may be incorrect)*

sic passim   *so throughout (used to show that a spelling, word, etc. has appeared in the same form throughout in a book, article, etc.)*

sine die   *without a day (appointed)*

sine dubio   *without doubt*

sine qua non   *a fundamental condition (literally, 'without which not . . .')*

status quo   *unchanged situation (literally, 'the state in which')*

stet   *an instruction to restore something which has been deleted (literally, 'let it stand')*

summa cum laude   *with greatest distinction (an academic award)*

terra firma   *the mainland; on solid ground, dry land*

vade mecum   *a useful handbook that one carries with oneself for constant reference; a pocket companion (literally, 'go with me')*

vice versa   *the other way around (literally, 'the position having been turned')*

vide   *see*

viva voce or viva   *an oral academic examination (literally, 'with the living voice')*

A

a, ab (+ ablative) ....

(also used as a prefix with verbs) ....

preposition ....

    from, away from, by ....

    (as prefix = away)

    abnormal, abscond, ...

    abstain (cf. 'teneo')

....

absum, abesse, afui[1]** ....

verb *(irreg.)*

    be absent, be away, be distant from ....

    absence, absent, absentee,

    absenteeism, absently ....

....

---

[1] The Eduqas specification does not include the perfect tense of 'sum' or its compounds.

accido, accidere, accidi
verb *(third)*
    happen
    accidence, accident, accidental,
    accidentally, accidented

....

....

....

....

accipio, accipere, accepi, acceptus
verb *(third/fourth)*
    accept, take in, receive
    accept, acceptability, acceptable,
    acceptance, accepted

....

....

....

....

ad (+ accusative)
(also used as a prefix with verbs)
preposition
    to, towards, at
    adapt, address, adhere, adhesion,
    adjective (cf. 'iacio'), advance,
    adverb (cf. 'verbum')

....

....

....

....

....

adiuvo, adiuvare, adiuvi, adiutus*
verb *(first)*
    help
    adjutancy, adjutant, adjuvancy,
    adjuvant

....

....

....

....

adsum, adesse, adfui[2]**

verb *(irreg.)*
> be here, be present
> *'adsum', adessive*

....

....

....

advenio, advenire, adveni

verb *(fourth)*
> arrive
> *advent, adventure, adventuresome,*
> *adventurous*

....

....

....

....

aedifico

aedifico, aedificare, aedificavi
aedificatus***

verb *(first)*
> build
> *edification, edifice, edificial, edify,*
> *edifying*

....

....

....

....

---

[2] The Eduqas specification does not include the perfect tense of 'sum' or its compounds.

ager, agri (masc.)***   ....

noun (2nd)

    field   ....

    agrichemical, agricultural, ...
    agriculture, agrobiology,
    agroecosystem   ....

ago, agere, egi, actus   ....

verb *(third)*

    do, act, drive   ....

    act, acting, action, active, actor, ...
    actressy, proactive (cf. 'pro')

              ....

alius, alia, aliud   ....

adjective/pronoun

    other, another, else   ....

    alias, alibi, alien, alienate, 'et alia' or   ....
    'et al.', 'inter alia' (cf. 'inter')

              ....

alter, altera, alterum   ....

adjective/pronoun

    the other, another, one (of two), ...
    the second (of two)

    alter, 'alter ego' (cf. 'ego'), altercate, ...
    alternate, alternative, altruistic

              ....

              ....

altus, alta, altum

....

adjective
   high, deep

....

   altitonant, altitude, altitudinal, alto

....

ambulo, ambulare, ambulavi

....

verb *(first)*
   walk

....

   amble, ambler, ambulance,
   ambulant, ambulatory,

....

   noctambulation,
   noctambulist (cf. 'nox')

....

....

amicus, amici (masc.)

....

noun (2nd)
   friend

....

   amicability, amicable, amicableness,
   amicably

....

....

amo, amare, amavi, amatus

....

verb *(first)*
   love, like

....

   Amanda, amiable, amorous
   (cf. 'amor')

....

....

amor, amoris (masc.)
noun (3rd)
   love
   Amanda, amiable, amorous
   (cf. 'amo')

ancilla, ancillae (fem.)
noun (1st)
   slave-girl, slave-woman
   ancillary

animus, animi (masc.)
noun (2nd)
   mind, spirit, soul
   animated, animatic, animation,
   animator, inanimate

annus, anni (masc.)
noun (2nd)
   year
   'anno domini' or 'A.D.' (cf. 'dominus'),
   annual, annualise, annually,
   annuitant, annuity, biennial,
   centennial (cf. 'centum'),
   novennial (cf. 'novem'),
   'per annum' or 'p.a.' (cf. 'per')

ante (+ accusative)*³
preposition
    before, in front of
    antecedent, antechamber, 'ante
    meridiem' or 'a.m.' (cf. 'dies'),
    anteprandial, 'raise/up the ante'

....

....

....

....

antea
adverb
    before, previously
    vide 'ante'

....

....

....

aperio, aperire, aperui, apertus*
verb *(fourth)*
    open
    aperient, aperitive, apert, aperture

....

....

....

appareo, apparere, apparui*
verb *(second)*
    appear
    apparency, apparent, apparently,
    apparition, apparitional, appearance

....

....

....

....

appropinquo, appropinquare,
appropinquavi (+ dative)
verb *(first)*
    approach, come near to
    appropinquate, appropinquation,
    appropinque, appropinquity

....

....

....

....

---

³ The OCR List does not include 'ante' although it does include 'antea', 'post' and 'postea'.

aqua, aquae (fem.)   ....
noun (1st)
   water   ....
   aqua, aquabatics,
   aquamarine (cf. 'mare'), ...
   aquanautics (cf. 'nauta'),
   aquaphobia, aquaplane, aquarium, ...
   aquatic, aqueduct (cf. 'duco')
                                          ....

arma, armorum (neut. pl.)***   ....
noun (2nd)
   arms, weapons   ....
   armament, armature, armed,
   armoury, arms   ....

                                          ....

ars, artis (fem.)***   ....
noun (3rd)
   art, skill   ....
   art, artefact, artful,
   artificial (cf. 'facio'), ...
   artistic, artistry, arty-farty   ....

ascendo, ascendere, ascendi, ascensus***   ....
verb *(third)*
   climb   ....
   ascend, ascendance, ascendancy,
   ascendent, ascension, ascent   ....

                                          ....

audax, (gen.) audacis
adjective
   bold, daring
   audacious, audaciously,
   audaciousness, audacity
   (cf. 'audeo')

....
....
....
....
....

audeo, audere, ausus sum***
verb *(second) (semi-deponent)*
   dare
   audacious, audaciously,
   audaciousness, audacity
   (cf. 'audax')

....
....
....
....
....

audio, audire, audivi, auditus
verb *(fourth)*
   hear, listen to
   audible, audiogram, audiograph,
   audiology, audiometer,
   audio-visual (cf. 'video'),
   auditory

....
....
....
....
....

aufero, auferre, abstuli, ablatus
verb *(irreg.)*
   take away, carry off, steal
   ablate, ablation, ablatitious,
   ablatival, ablative

....
....
....
....

auxilium, auxilii (neut.)*** ....
noun (2nd)
   help ....
   auxiliar, auxiliary ....

....

B

bellum

bellum, belli (neut.) ....
noun (2nd) ....
   war
   Bellatrix, belligerence, belligerency, ...
   belligerent, belligerently (cf. 'gero')
....

bene　　　　　　　　　　　　　..............................
adverb
 well　　　　　　　　　　　　..............................
 Benedict (cf. 'dico'), benefaction,
 benefactor, beneficial, beneficiary,　..............................
 benefit (cf. 'facio'),
 benevolent (cf. 'volo'),　　　　..............................
 'nota bene' or 'N.B.',
 omnibenevolent (cf. 'omnis')　　..............................

benignus, benigna, benignum*　　..............................
adjective
 kind, generous　　　　　　　..............................
 benign, benignancy, benignant,
 benignantly, benignity, benignly　..............................

 　　　　　　　　　　　　　..............................

bibo, bibere, bibi　　　　　　..............................
verb *(third)*
 drink　　　　　　　　　　　..............................
 bib, bibacious, bibation, bibber,
 imbibe, imbibition　　　　　..............................

 　　　　　　　　　　　　　..............................

bonus, bona, bonum　　　　　..............................
adjective
 good　　　　　　　　　　　..............................
 'bona fide', bonus
 　　　　　　　　　　　　　..............................

 　　　　　　　　　　　　　..............................

brevis, breve ....
adjective ....
   short, brief
   abbreviate, abbreviation, ...
   brevipennate, brevity, briefcase,
   briefs ....

....

C

cado, cadere, cecidi, casus
verb *(third)*
    fall
    cadence, cadenced, cadent,
    cadential, cadenza, case

....
....
....
....

caelum, caeli (neut.)
noun (2nd)
    sky, heaven
    celeste, celestial, celestially,
    celestite, coelostat

....
....
....
....

canis, canis (masc.)*
noun (3rd)
    dog
    canine, caninity, Canis Major,
    Canis Minor

....
....
....
....

capio, capere, cepi, captus
verb *(third/fourth)*
    take, catch, capture, make (a plan)
    capsule, caption, capture, conception,
    contraception (cf. 'contra'),
    inception (cf. 'in')
    (cf. 'captivus')

captivus, captivi (masc.)***
noun (2nd)
    captive, prisoner
    captivate, captivation, captive,
    captivity, captor, capturer
    (cf. 'capio')

caput, capitis (neut.)
noun (3rd)
    head
    capital, capitalise, capitulate,
    captain, decapitate, 'per capita',
    triceps (cf. 'tres')

carus, cara, carum*
adjective
    dear
    caress, caressing, caressingly,
    caressive, cherish, cherished

castra, castrorum (neut. pl.)***
noun (2nd)
    camp
    castle; 'caster', 'cester' and 'chester'
    in names of places in Britain,
    e.g. Chester, Cirencester,
    Grantchester, Lancaster, Manchester,
    Winchester

....
....
....
....
....
....

celer, celeris, celere
adjective
    quick, fast
    accelerate, acceleration, accelerator,
    accelerometer, celerity

....
....
....
....

celo, celare, celavi, celatus
verb *(first)*
    hide
    conceal, concealable, concealer,
    concealment

....
....
....
....

cena, cenae (fem.)
noun (1st)
    dinner, meal
    cenacle

....
....
....
....

centum ....

number (indecl.)

    100 ....

    centenary, centennial (cf. 'annus'),
centimetre, centipede (cf. 'pes'), ...
century, 'per centum' or
'per cent' (cf. 'per'), ...
quatercentenary (cf. 'quattuor'),
quincentenary (cf. 'quinque') ....

....

ceteri, ceterae, cetera ....

adjective/pronoun

    the rest, the others ....

    'ceteris paribus' or 'cet. par.',
    'et cetera' or 'etc.' ....

....

cibus

cibus, cibi (masc.) ....

noun (2nd)

    food ....

    cibation ....

circum (+ accusative)
(also used as a prefix with verbs)[4]**
preposition
  around
  circle, circuit,
  circumambulate (cf. 'ambulo'),
  circumference (cf. 'fero'),
  circumnavigate (cf. 'navigo'),
  circumvent (cf. 'venio'), circus

civis, civis (masc. and fem.)
noun (3rd)
  citizen
  civic, civil, civilian, civilisation,
  civilised, civility

clamo, clamare, clamavi, clamatus
verb *(first)*
  shout
  clamorous, clamorously, clamourer,
  exclaim, exclamation
  (cf. 'clamor')

clamor, clamoris (masc.)
noun (3rd)
  shout, shouting, noise
  clamorousness, clamour,
  exclamational,
  exclamative, exclamatory
  (cf. 'clamo')

---

[4] The OCR List does not include its use as a prefix with verbs.

clarus, clara, clarum****
adjective
    famous, clear, distinguished, bright
    Claire, Clara, Clare, clarify, clarinet,
    clarion, clarity

....
....
....
....

cogito, cogitare, cogitavi, cogitatus
verb *(first)*
    think, consider
    cogitate, cogitation, cogitative,
    incogitable

....
....
....
....

cognosco, cognoscere, cognovi, cognitus
verb *(third)*
    get to know, find out
    cognition, cognitive, cognosce,
    incognito, recognise, recognition

....
....
....
....

cogo, cogere, coegi, coactus
verb *(third)*
    force, compel
    coact, coaction, coactive

....
....
....
....

comes, comitis (masc. and fem.)
noun (3rd)
    comrade, companion
    comital, comitative, comitatus

....
....
....

conficio, conficere, confeci, confectus
verb *(third/fourth)*
    finish; wear out, exhaust
    confect, confection, confectionary,
    confectioner, confectionery

....
....
....
....

conor, conari, conatus sum
verb *(first) (deponent)*
    try
    conation, conative, conatus

....
....
....

consilium, consilii (neut.)
noun (2nd)
    plan, idea, advice
    consilience, consilient

....
....
....

**conspicio, conspicere, conspexi,
conspectus**
verb *(third/fourth)*
    catch sight of, notice
    conspectus, conspicuity, conspicuous,
    conspicuously, conspicuousness,
    inconspicuous

....
....
....
....
....

**constituo, constituere, constitui,
constitutus**
verb *(third)*
    decide
    constituency, constituent, constitute,
    constitution, constitutional,
    constitutively

....
....
....
....
....

consul, consulis (masc.)***   ....

noun (3rd)
    consul   ....
    consul, consulage, consular, consulate, ...
    consulship

....

consumo, consumere, consumpsi, ...
consumptus

verb *(third)*   ....
    eat   ....
    consumable, consume, consumer,
    consumerism, consumption   ....

contra (+ accusative)   ....

preposition
    against   ....
    contraband, contraception (cf. 'capio'), ...
    contradict (cf. 'dico'),
    contraflow, contraindicate, ...
    contrary, contrast,
    contravene (cf. 'venio'), ...
    'pros and cons' (cf. 'pro')

....

convenio, convenire, conveni, conventus[5]   ....

verb *(fourth)*
    come together, gather, meet   ....
    convene, convenience, convenient, ...
    convenor, convent, convention,
    reconvene (cf. 're' and 'venio')   ....

---

[5] Although 'convenio' does not appear as a separate entry on the Eduqas List, learners are expected to be familiar with it as it is a common compound of 'cum' and 'venio' which are both on the Eduqas List. See notes to Appendix One.

copiae, copiarum (fem. pl.)***   ....

noun (1st)

   forces, troops   ....

   copious, copiously, copiousness   ....

corpus, corporis (neut.)   ....

noun (3rd)

   body   ....

   corporal, corporate, corporation, ...
   incorporate, incorporation

   ....

cras***   ....

adverb

   tomorrow   ....

   procrastinate, procrastination, ...
   procrastinative, procrastinator,
   procrastinatory   ....

credo, credere, credidi, creditus   ....
(+ dative)

verb *(third)*   ....

   believe, trust, have faith in   ....

   credence, credentials, credibility, ...
   credible, incredible, incredulous

crudelis, crudele   ....

adjective

   cruel   ....

   cruel, cruelly, cruelness, cruelty   ....

cum (+ ablative)
(also used as a prefix with verbs as col- /
com- / con- / cor-)[6]*
preposition
    with (as prefix = together)
    'summa cum laude' (cf. 'summus'
    and 'laudo'),
    as a combining form, e.g. 'kitchen-
    cum-dining-room', 'vade mecum'

cupio, cupere, cupivi, cupitus[7]**
verb *(third/fourth)*
    want, desire
    Cupid, Cupid's bow, cupidinous,
    cupidity

cura, curae (fem.)
noun (1st)
    care, worry
    curacy, curate, curator, curatorship,
    cure, incurable, pedicure (cf. 'pes'),
    sinecure (cf. 'sine')
    (cf. 'curo')

curo, curare, curavi, curatus*
verb *(first)*
    look after, care for, supervise
    curate, curator, curatorial,
    curatorship
    (cf. 'cura')

---

[6] The OCR List does not include its use as a prefix with verbs.

[7] 'cupitus' is not included on the Eduqas List, for historical reasons.

curro, currere, cucurri, cursus   ....

verb *(third)*   ....

    run

    currency, current, cursive, cursively, ...
    cursor, cursory, recur (cf. 're')

                                      ....

custodio, custodire, custodivi,
custoditus***   ....

verb *(fourth)*   ....

    guard

    custode, custodial, custodian,
    custodianship, custodier, custody   ....
    (cf. 'custos')

                                        ....

custos, custodis (masc. and fem.)   ....

noun (3rd)   ....

    guard

    custode, custodial, custodian,
    custodianship, custodier, custody   ....
    (cf. 'custodio')

                                        ....

D

de (+ ablative)
(also used as a prefix with verbs)[8]*
preposition
 from, down from; about
 (as prefix = down)
 deactivate, derivative, descend,
 descendant (cf. 'descendo'),
 descent, deseed, desensitise

....
....
....
....
....
....

dea, deae (fem.)
noun (1st)
 goddess
 deific, deification, deiform, deify,
 deity
 (cf. 'deus')

....
....
....
....

---

[8] The OCR List does not include its use as a prefix with verbs.

debeo, debere, debui, debitus
verb *(second)*
   owe, ought, should, must
   debenture, debit, debt, debtee, debtor,
   indebted

....

....

....

....

decem
number (indecl.)
   ten
   decagon, December,
   decennary (cf. 'annus'),
   decimal, decimate, decimetre

....

....

....

....

defendo, defendere, defendi,
defensus***
verb *(third)*
   defend
   defence, defenceless, defendant,
   defender, defensive, indefensible

....

....

....

....

deleo, delere, delevi, deletus
verb *(second)*
   destroy
   delete, deletion, deletive, deletory

....

....

....

descendo, descendere, descendi,
descensus***
verb *(third)*
   go down, come down
   descend, descendable, descending,
   descension, descent
   (cf. 'de')

....

....

....

....

....

despero, desperare, desperavi, ...
desperatus*
verb *(first)* ....
   despair ....
   despairful, despairing, desperate,
   desperateness, desperation ....
   (cf. 'spero' and 'spes')
   ....

deus, dei (masc.) ....
noun (2nd)
   god ....
   deific, deification, deiform, deify,
   deity ....
   (cf. 'dea')
   ....

dico, dicere, dixi, dictus ....
verb *(third)*
   say, speak, tell ....
   Benedict (cf. 'bene'),
   contradict (cf. 'contra'), ...
   dictate, dictation, diction,
   dictionary, dictum ....
   ....

dies, diei (masc.)[9] ....
noun (5th)
   day ....
   'ante meridiem' or 'a.m.' (cf. 'ante'),
   'carpe diem', diarise, diary, diurnal, ...
   'post meridiem' or 'p.m.' (cf. 'post'),
   quotidian (cf. 'quot') ....
   ....

---

[9] 'dies' can also be feminine (when it refers to a special day) but both the OCR List and the Eduqas List include it as masculine only.

difficilis, difficile   ....
adjective
   difficult   ....
   difficult, difficulty   ....

diligens, (gen.) diligentis***   ....
adjective
   careful   ....
   diligence, diligent, diligently   ....

....

dirus, dira, dirum   ....
adjective
   dreadful   ....
   dire, direful, direfully, direfulness, ...
   direness

....

discedo, discedere, discessi   ....
verb *(third)*
   depart, leave   ....
   decease, deceased   ....

diu   ....
adverb
   for a long time   ....
   diuturnal, diuturnity   ....

do, dare, dedi, datus
verb *(first)*
>give
>*data, dative, donate, donation,*
>*donee, donor*
>*(cf. 'donum')*

....

....

....

....

doceo, docere, docui, doctus***
verb *(second)*
>teach
>*doctor, doctoral, doctorate, doctrine,*
>*document, documentary*

....

....

....

....

domina, dominae (fem.)
noun (1st)
>mistress
>*dominant, dominate, domination,*
>*domineer, dominion, domino*
>*(cf. 'dominus')*

....

....

....

....

dominus, domini (masc.)
noun (2nd)
>master
>*'anno domini' or 'A.D.' (cf. 'annus'),*
>*dominant, dominate, domination,*
>*domineer, dominion, domino*
>*(cf. 'domina')*

....

....

....

....

domus, domus (fem.)[10]   ....
noun (4th)
   home, house   ....
   domestic, domesticated, domesticity,
   domicile, domiciliary   ....

....

donum, doni (neut.)   ....
noun (2nd)
   gift, present   ....
   donate, donation, donee, donor
   (cf. 'do')   ....

....

dormio

dormio, dormire, dormivi   ....
verb *(fourth)*
   sleep   ....
   dormant, dormer, dormitive,
   dormitory, dormouse, dormy   ....

....

---

[10] **domi** = at home.

duco, ducere, duxi, ductus   ....
verb *(third)*
   lead, take   ....
   aqueduct (cf. 'aqua'), duct, ductile, ...
   ductility, viaduct (cf. 'via')
   (cf. 'dux')   ....

duo, duae, duo   ....
number
   two   ....
   dual, duathlon, duel, duet, duo   ....

durus, dura, durum*   ....
adjective
   hard, harsh   ....
   durability, durable, duraluminium, ...
   duration, endurance, endure
        ....

dux, ducis (masc.)   ....
noun (3rd)
   leader   ....
   duct, ducted, ductless, ductileness, ...
   ducting
   (cf. 'duco')   ....

E

e, ex (+ ablative)
(also used as a prefix with verbs)
preposition
    from, out, out of
    ex-, e.g. ex-boyfriend, ex-directory,
    ex-employer, etc.,
    'exeat' (cf. 'eo'),
    exhale, exit (cf. 'eo'),
    exude

....
....
....
....
....
....

effugio, effugere, effugi
verb *(third/fourth)*
    escape
    fugitive, fugitively, fugitiveness,
    refuge, refugee (cf. 're')
    (cf. 'fugio')

....
....
....
....

ego, mei
pronoun
    I, me
    (N.B. 'me' is a good example of an accusative
    in English)
    'alter ego' (cf. 'alter'),
    ego, egocentric, egoist, egomania,
    egotism,
    'vade mecum' (cf. 'cum')

egredior, egredi, egressus sum
verb *(third/fourth) (deponent)*
    go out
    egress, egression, egressive

emo, emere, emi, emptus
verb *(third)*
    buy
    'caveat emptor', emption, pre-empt

eo, ire, i(v)i
verb *(irreg.)*
    go
    circuit (cf. 'circum'),
    'exeat', exit (cf. 'e, ex')

epistula, epistulae (fem.)
noun *(1st)*
    letter
    epistle, epistolarian, epistoler,
    epistolet, epistolography

equus

equus, equi (masc.)   ....
noun (2nd)
   horse   ....
   equestrian, equine
            ....

exercitus, exercitus (masc.)***   ....
noun (4th)
   army   ....
   exercisable, exercise, exercitation
            ....

exspecto, exspectare, exspectavi, ...
exspectatus
verb *(first)*   ....
   wait for, expect
   expect, expectably, expectancy, ...
   expectation, expected
            ....

F

fabula, fabulae (fem.)[11]*
noun (1st)
   story
   fable, fabled, fabulous, fabulousness

....

....

....

facilis, facile
adjective
   easy
   facile, facilitate, facilitation, facilitator,
   facilities

....

....

....

....

facio, facere, feci, factus
verb *(third/fourth)*
   make, do
   artefact (cf. 'ars'),
   benefactor (cf. 'bene'),
   fact, faction, factitious, factor, factory,
   factual

....

....

....

....

---

[11] 'fabula' is not currently in the Eduqas Latin to English DVL but it does appear in the Eduqas English to Latin DVL. Eduqas has advised that, for consistency, it intends to amend the Latin to English DVL to include 'fabula' at the next syllabus update.

faveo, favere, favi, fautus (+ dative)****

verb *(second)*
   favour, support
   favour, favourable, favoured,
   favourite, favouritism

....
....
....
....

felix, (gen.) felicis****

adjective
   fortunate, happy
   felicitate, felicitations, feliciter,
   felicitous, Felicity, Felix

....
....
....
....

femina, feminae (fem.)

noun (1st)
   woman
   feminal, feminine, femininity,
   feminise, feminism

....
....
....
....

fero, ferre, tuli, latus

verb *(irreg.)*
   bring, carry, bear
   'confer' or 'cf.', feretory, relate,
   relationship, relative,
   transfer (cf. 'trans')

....
....
....
....

ferox, (gen.) ferocis
adjective
    fierce, ferocious
    ferocious, ferociousness, ferocity

....

....

....

festino, festinare, festinavi
verb *(first)*
    hurry
    festinate, festinately, festination

....

....

....

fidelis, fidele
adjective
    faithful, loyal
    fidelity, infidelity,
    'semper fidelis' (cf. 'semper')

....

....

....

....

filia, filiae (fem.)
noun (1st)
    daughter
    affiliate, affiliation, filial, filially
    (cf. 'filius')

....

....

....

....

filius, filii (masc.)
noun (2nd)
    son
    affiliate, affiliation, filial, filially
    (cf. 'filia')

....

....

....

....

flumen

flumen, fluminis (neut.)
noun (3rd)
  river
  flume

....

....

....

....

forte
adverb
  by chance
  fortuitous, fortuitously,
  fortuitousness, fortuity, fortune

....

....

....

....

fortis, forte
adjective
  brave
  fortifiable, fortification, fortified,
  fortifier, fortify, fortifying

....

....

....

....

forum, fori (neut.)
noun (2nd)
  forum, marketplace
  forum

....
....
....
....

frango, frangere, fregi, fractus*
verb *(third)*
  break
  fract, fraction, fractious,
  fractography, fracture, fracking

....
....
....
....

frater, fratris (masc.)
noun (3rd)
  brother
  fraternal, fraternisation, fraternise,
  fraternity, fratricide
  (cf. 'mater', 'pater' and 'soror')

....
....
....
....

frustra
adverb
  in vain
  frustrate, frustrated, frustrating,
  frustratingly, frustration

....
....
....
....

fugio, fugere, fugi
verb *(third/fourth)*
  run away, flee
  fugitive, fugitively, fugitiveness,
  refuge, refugee (cf. 're')
  (cf. 'effugio')

....
....
....
....

G

gaudeo

gaudeo, gaudere, gavisus sum***   ....
verb *(second) (semi-deponent)*   ....
   be pleased, rejoice   ....
   gaud, gaudery, gaudiness, gaudy,
   gaudy-day/night
   (cf. gaudium)   ....

gaudium, gaudii (neut.)***
noun (2nd)
   joy, pleasure
   gaud, gaudery, gaudiness, gaudy,
   gaudy-day/night
   (cf. gaudeo)

....

....

....

....

gens, gentis (fem.)***
noun (3rd)
   family, tribe, race, people
   genitive, gentile, gentilic, gentilism,
   gentilitian

....

....

....

....

gero, gerere, gessi, gestus
verb *(third)*
   wear (clothes), wage (war)
   belligerent (cf. 'bellum'),
   gestate, gestation, gestational,
   gestative

....

....

....

....

gladius, gladii (masc.)
noun (2nd)
   sword
   gladiate, gladiator, gladiatorial,
   gladiatorship, gladiolus

....

....

....

....

gravis, grave
adjective
   heavy, serious
   grave, gravimeter, gravitas,
   gravitate, gravitational,
   gravity

....

....

....

....

H

habito, habitare, habitavi, habitatus
verb *(first)*
    live (in), inhabit, dwell
    habit, habitat, habitation, habitual,
    habitudinal, inhabitable

....

....

....

....

hodie
adverb
    today
    hodiernal

....

....

....

homo, hominis (masc.)
noun (3rd)
    man, human being
    'homo sapiens', human, humane,
    humanist, humanitarian, humanity

....

....

....

....

hora, horae (fem.)   ....

noun (1st)
   hour   ....
   horologe, horologer, horologist,
   horology, horometry, horoscope   ....

....

hortor, hortari, hortatus sum***   ....

verb *(first) (deponent)*
   encourage, urge   ....
   exhort, exhortation, hortation,
   hortative, hortatory   ....

....

hortus

hortus, horti (masc.)   ....

noun (2nd)
   garden   ....
   horticultural, horticulturalist,
   horticulture   ....

....

hostis, hostis (masc.)   ....
noun (3rd)   ....
   enemy
   hostile, hostilely, hostilities, hostility   ....

I

N.B. 'i' becomes 'j' in many derivatives as the letter 'j' did not exist in the Roman alphabet; so 'Iulius Caesar' becomes Julius Caesar.

iaceo, iacere, iacui
verb *(second)*
    lie (positional)
    adjacent, jacent

....

....

....

....

iacio, iacere, ieci, iactus (in compounds -icio)
verb *(third/fourth)*
    throw
    adjective (cf. 'ad'), ejaculation, eject (cf. 'e, ex'), interject (cf. 'inter'), jaculator, object, projection (cf. 'pro'), subject (cf. 'sub')

....

....

....

....

....

....

ianua, ianuae (fem.)   ....
noun (1st)   ....
   door   ....
   janitor, janitorial, janitorship,
   janitress, janitrix   ....

                             ....

ibi   ....
adverb   ....
   there   ....
   'ibidem' or 'ib.' or 'ibid.' (cf. 'idem')
                             ....

idem, eadem, idem*   ....
pronoun   ....
   the same   ....
   'ibidem' or 'ib.' or 'ibid.' (cf. 'ibi'),
   'idem' or 'id', ...
   idempotency, idempotent
   (cf. 'possum'), ...
   identical, identify, identity,
   'semper idem' (cf. 'semper')   ....

                             ....

ignis, ignis (masc.)*   ....
noun (3rd)   ....
   fire   ....
   igneous, ignescent, ignipotent, ignite,
   ignition   ....

                             ....

imperator, imperatoris (masc.)
noun (3rd)
    emperor; general, leader, commander
    empire, imperial, imperialism,
    imperialist, imperialistic, imperious
    (cf. 'imperium' and 'impero')

....

....

....

....

imperium, imperii (neut.)
noun (2nd)
    empire, power, command
    empire, imperial, imperialism,
    imperialist, imperialistic, imperious
    (cf. 'imperator' and 'impero')

....

....

....

....

impero, imperare, imperavi, imperatus
(+ dative)
verb *(first)*
    order, command
    empire, imperative, imperial,
    imperialism, imperialist, imperiality,
    imperious
    (cf. 'imperator' and 'imperium')

....

....

....

....

....

in (+ ablative)
(also used as a prefix with verbs)
preposition
    in, on
    in, and as a prefix to many
    words, e.g. inception (cf. 'capio'),
    incite, include
    (cf. 'in (+ accusative)')

....

....

....

....

....

in (+ accusative)
(also used as a prefix with verbs)
preposition
    into, onto
    into, and as a prefix to many words,
    e.g. incorporate, incubate, invade
    (cf. 'in (+ ablative)')

....
....
....
....
....

incendo, incendere, incendi, incensus
verb *(third)*
    burn, set on fire
    incendiary, incendivity, incense
    (verb and noun), incensed

....
....
....
....

infelix, (gen.) infelicis
adjective
    unlucky, unhappy
    infelicitous, infelicity

....
....
....

ingredior, ingredi, ingressus sum
verb *(third/fourth) (deponent)*
    enter
    ingredient, ingress, ingression,
    ingressive

....
....
....
....

inimicus, inimici (masc.)***
noun (2nd)
    enemy
    inimical, inimicality, inimically,
    inimicalness, inimicitous

....
....
....
....

insula

insula, insulae (fem.)   ....
noun (1st)
    island; block of flats   ....
    insular, insularism, insulate, ...
    insulation, insulator, peninsula,
    peninsular (cf. 'paene')   ....

intellego, intellegere, intellexi, intellectus   ....
verb *(third)*
    understand, realise   ....
    intellect, intellectual, intelligence,
    intelligent, intelligible   ....

    ....

inter (+ accusative)   ....
preposition
    among, between   ....
    'inter alia' (cf. 'alius'), interact,
    intercept (cf. 'capio'), intercom, ...
    interim, interlude, interrupt
    (cf. 'interea')   ....

    ....

interea
adverb
    meanwhile
    vide 'inter'

intro, intrare, intravi, intratus
verb *(first)*
    enter, go in
    enter, entering, entrance, entrant

invenio, invenire, inveni, inventus
verb *(fourth)*
    find
    invent, invention, inventive,
    inventiveness, inventory

invito, invitare, invitavi, invitatus***
verb *(first)*
    invite
    invitation, invite, invitee,
    inviting, invitingness

ipse, ipsa, ipsum***
pronoun
    himself, herself, itself, *pl.* themselves
    ipselateral, 'ipso facto'

ira, irae (fem.)
noun (1st)
    anger
    iracundity, irascibility, irascibly,
    irateness, ire
    (cf. 'iratus')

iratus, irata, iratum
adjective
    angry
    iracundulous, irascible, irate,
    irately, ire, irefulness
    (cf. 'ira')

is, ea, id
pronoun
    he, she, it, *pl.* they; that, *pl.* those
    'id est' or 'i.e.'

iter, itineris (neut.)
noun (3rd)
    journey
    itineracy, itinerant, itinerantly,
    itinerary, itinerate

iterum
adverb
    again
    iterance, iterate, iterative, reiterate
    (cf. 're-'), reiteration

iubeo, iubere, iussi, iussus   ....
verb *(second)*
   order   ....
   jussive   ....

iuvenis, iuvenis (masc.)   ....
noun (3rd)
   young man   ....
   juvenile, juvenilely, juvenileness, ...
   juvenilise, juvenility
        ....

L

labor, laboris (masc.)
noun (3rd)
    work, toil
    laborious, labour, labourer,
    labourism, labourist
    (cf. 'laboro')

....

....

....

....

laboro, laborare, laboravi
verb *(first)*
    work, toil
    laboriously, laboriousness, labour,
    laboured, laboursome
    (cf. 'labor')

....

....

....

....

lacrimo, lacrimare, lacrimavi
verb *(first)*
    weep, cry
    lacrimal, lacrimary, lacrimation,
    lacrimose, lacrimosity

....

....

....

....

laetus, laeta, laetum   ....
adjective
  happy   ....
  laetare, Letitia   ....

latus, lata, latum*   ....
adjective
  wide   ....
  dilatable, dilatant, dilate, dilated, ...
  dilation, latitude

  ....

laudo, laudare, laudavi, laudatus   ....
verb *(first)*
  praise   ....
  applaud, applause, laud, laudable, ...
  laudatory

  ....

legatus, legati (masc.)*   ....
noun (2nd)
  commander   ....
  legate, legateship, legatine, legation   ....
  (cf. 'legio')

  ....

legio, legionis (fem.)   ....
noun (3rd)
  legion   ....
  legion, legionary, legionnaire   ....
  (cf. 'legatus')

  ....

lego

lego, legere, legi, lectus
verb *(third)*
    read; choose
    elect, election, elective, lector, lecture,
    lecturer, re-elect (cf. 're')

....

....

....

....

lente[12]*
indecl.
    slowly
    lentic, relent, relentless, relentlessly
    (cf. 'lentus')

....

....

....

....

lentus, lenta, lentum***
adjective
    slow
    relent, relenting, relentless,
    relentlessly
    (cf. 'lente')

....

....

....

....

---

[12] Although 'lente' does not appear as a separate entry on the OCR List, candidates are expected to be familiar with it as it is a regular adverb formed from the adjective 'lentus' which is on the OCR List. See notes to Appendix Two.

liber, libri (masc.)***   ....

noun (2nd)   ....
   book   ....
   librarian, librarianship, library

libero, liberare, liberavi, liberatus   ....

verb *(first)*   ....
   free, set free
   deliver, deliverance, liberate, ...
   liberation, libertarian, liberty
   (cf. 'libertus')   ....

libertus, liberti (masc.)   ....

noun (2nd)   ....
   freedman, ex-slave
   libertarianism, liberticide, ...
   libertinage,
   libertine, libertinism, liberty   ....
   (cf. 'libero')

                                ....

locus, loci (masc.) (pl. is neut.: loca)   ....

noun (2nd)   ....
   place
   local, locality, location, locum, locus   ....

longus, longa, longum   ....

adjective   ....
   long
   long, longevity, longing, longitude, ...
   longwise

                                ....

loquor, loqui, locutus sum
verb *(third) (deponent)*
    speak, talk
    elocution, eloquent,
    loquacious, loquacity,
    magniloquent (cf. 'magnus'),
    pauciloquent (cf. 'pauci')

lux, lucis (fem.)
noun (3rd)
    light, daylight
    elucidate, lucency, lucid,
    lucidity, Lucinda, luxmeter,
    noctilucent (cf. 'nox'),
    translucent (cf. 'trans')

M

magnus, magna, magnum
adjective
    big, large, great
    magnificence, magnificent,
    magnifier, magnify,
    magniloquent (cf. 'loquor'),
    magnitude, Magnus

....

....

....

....

....

maior, maius
adjective (comparative of 'magnus')
    bigger, larger, greater
    major, majority, majorly, majorship

....

....

....

malus, mala, malum
adjective
    evil, bad
    maleficent, malice, malign,
    malnourish, malpractice

....

....

....

....

maneo, manere, mansi
verb *(second)*
    remain, stay
    manse, mansion, mansionary,
    remain, remainder

....

....

....

....

manus, manus (fem.)
noun (4th)
    hand; group of people
    manual, manually, manufacture,
    manufacturer (cf. 'facio'),
    manuscript (cf. 'scribo')

....

....

....

....

mare

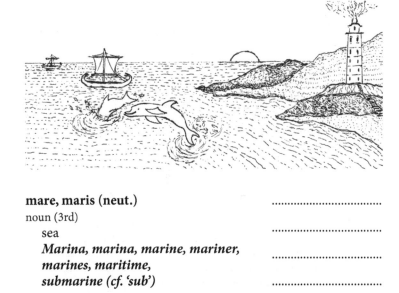

mare, maris (neut.)
noun (3rd)
    sea
    Marina, marina, marine, mariner,
    marines, maritime,
    submarine (cf. 'sub')

....

....

....

....

maritus, mariti (masc.)
noun (2nd)
    husband
    marital, maritally

....

....

....

mater, matris (fem.)
noun (3rd)
    mother
    'alma mater', maternal,
    maternalism, maternalistic,
    maternally, maternity
    (cf. 'frater', 'pater' and 'soror')

....

....

....

....

maxime[13]
adverb
    very greatly
    vide 'maximus'

....

....

....

maximus, maxima, maximum
adjective (superlative of 'magnus')
    biggest, greatest, very big, very great
    maximal, maximalist, Maximilian,
    maximise, maximum, Maxine

....

....

....

....

---

[13] Although 'maxime' does not appear as a separate entry on the Eduqas List, learners are expected to be familiar with it as it is an adverb formed from the adjective 'maximus' which is on the Eduqas List. See notes to Appendix One.

    Eduqas has explained that 'minime' is included on the Eduqas List because it is regularly used to mean 'no', which is a special usage of this form and quite distinct from standard superlative usages. By contrast, 'maxime' is only used with its standard meanings, and so is not listed separately.

medius, media, medium
adjective
    middle (of)
    media, medial, median, mediation,
    Mediterranean (cf. 'terra'), medium

....
....
....
....

melior, melius
adjective (comparative of 'bonus')
    better
    ameliorate, meliorate, melioration,
    melioristic, meliority

....
....
....
....

meus, mea, meum
pronoun
    my
    'mea culpa'

....
....
....

miles, militis (masc.)
noun (3rd)
    soldier
    militant, militarise, military, militia

....
....
....

mille, pl. milia
number
    1,000
    millennium (cf. 'annus'), millennial,
    millimetre, millipede (cf. 'pes'),
    millisecond

....
....
....
....

minime
adverb
   very little, least; no
   vide 'minimus'

minimus, minima, minimum
adjective (superlative of 'parvus')
   very little, smallest
   miniature (mini-), minibus, minim,
   minimalist, minimise, minimum

minor, minus
adjective (comparative of 'parvus')
   smaller, less
   minor, minority, minus, minuscule,
   minutiae

miror, mirari, miratus sum*
verb *(first) (deponent)*
   wonder at, admire
   admirably, admiration, miracle,
   miraculous, mirage, Miranda

miser, misera, miserum
adjective
   miserable, wretched, sad
   miser, miserable, miserably, miserly,
   misery

mitto, mittere, misi, missus
verb *(third)*
    send
    permit (cf. 'per'), premise, remiss,
    remit, remittance, remitting

    ....
    ....
    ....
    ....

modus, modi (masc.)
noun (2nd)
    manner, way, kind
    modal, mode, modish, module,
    'modus operandi'

    ....
    ....
    ....
    ....

moneo, monere, monui, monitus***
verb *(second)*
    warn, advise
    admonish, admonishment, monition,
    monitor, monitory

    ....
    ....
    ....
    ....

mons, montis (masc.)
noun (3rd)
    mountain
    mount, mountain, mountaineering,
    mountainous, mounted

    ....
    ....
    ....
    ....

morior, mori, mortuus sum
verb *(third/fourth) (deponent)*
    die
    immortal, immortalise, immortality,
    mortal, mortality
    (cf. 'mors')

    ....
    ....
    ....
    ....

mors, mortis (fem.)
noun (3rd)
    death
    mortalise, mortally, mortuary,
    post-mortem (cf. 'post')
    (cf. 'morior')

moveo, movere, movi, motus***
verb *(second)*
    move
    movable, move, movement, movie,
    moving

multo
adverb
    much, by much
    vide 'multus'

multus, multa, multum
adjective
    much, *pl.* many
    multi-, multicultural, multilinguist,
    multimedia, multiple,
    multiplication, multitude

murus, muri (masc.)
noun (2nd)
    wall
    mural, muralist, muriform

N

narro, narrare, narravi, narratus
verb *(first)*
    tell, relate
    narratable, narrate, narration,
    narrative, narrator

....
....
....
....

nauta, nautae (masc.)
noun (1st)
    sailor
    aquanautics (cf. 'aqua'), nautical,
    nautically, nautics

....
....
....
....

navigo, navigare, navigavi
verb *(first)*
    sail
    circumnavigate (cf. 'circum'),
    navigability, navigable, navigate,
    navigation, navigational, satnav
    (cf. 'navis')

....
....
....
....

navis, navis (fem.)   ....
noun (3rd)   ....
   ship
   navaid, naval, navalism, navy   ....
   (cf. 'navigo')
                                        ....

necesse*   ....
indecl.   ....
   necessary
   necessarily, necessitate, necessitous, ...
   necessity
                                          ....

nescio, nescire, nescivi   ....
verb *(fourth)*   ....
   not know
   nescience, nescient   ....
   (cf. 'scio')
                                          ....

nihil (neut.)   ....
noun *(irreg.)*   ....
   nothing
   annihilate, annihilation, nihilism, ...
   nihilist, nil, nilpotent (cf. 'possum')
                                          ....

nolo, nolle, nolui   ....
verb *(irreg.)*   ....
   not want, refuse
   nolition   ....
   (cf. 'volo')
                                          ....

nomen, nominis (neut.)
noun (3rd)
    name
    denomination, nomenclature,
    nominal, nominative, nominee, noun

non
adverb
    not
    non-, e.g. non-drip, non-executive,
    non-mover, non-profitmaking,
    nonsense

nos, nostrum
pronoun
    we, us
    'inter nos', nostrum

novem
number (indecl.)
    nine
    November, novenary,
    novennial (cf. 'annus')

novus, nova, novum
adjective
    new
    novate, novation, novel, novice,
    renovation

nox

nox, noctis (fem.)   ....
noun (3rd)
 night   ....
 noctambulation, noctambulist
 (cf. 'ambulo'), noctilucent (cf. 'lux'), ...
 noctivagant, nocturnal, nocturne   ....

nullus, nulla, nullum   ....
adjective
 not any, no ...   .
 null, nullification, nullifidian,
 nullify, nullity   ....

                                    ....

nuntio, nuntiare, nuntiavi, nuntiatus   ....
verb *(first)*
 announce, report   ....
 announce, announcement,
 announcer, renounce, ...
 renounceable, renouncement
 (cf. 'nuntius')   ....

                                    ....

nuntius, nuntii (masc.)   ....

noun (2nd)   ....

    messenger, message, news   ....

    announce, announcement,

    announcer, renounceable, ...

    renouncement, renouncer

    (cf. 'nuntio')   ....

    ....

O

octo
number (indecl.)
   eight
   oct-, octagon, octave, October,
   octopus, octuplet

....

....

....

....

offero, offerre, obtuli, oblatus
verb *(irreg.)*
   offer
   oblate, offer, offeree, offering,
   offeror, offertory,
   proffer (cf. 'pro')

....

....

....

....

omnis, omne
adjective
   all, every
   omnibenevolent (cf. 'bene'), omnibus,
   omnificent (cf. 'facio'), omnipotent
   (cf. 'possum'), omnipresent (cf. 'sum'),
   omniscient (cf. 'scio'), omnivore

....

....

....

....

opprimo, opprimere, oppressi,
oppressus***
verb *(third)*
   crush, overwhelm
   oppress, oppression, oppressive,
   oppressiveness, oppressor

oppugno, oppugnare, oppugnavi,
oppugnatus
verb *(first)*
   attack
   oppugn, oppugnancy, oppugnant,
   oppugner
   (cf. 'pugno')

optimus, optima, optimum
adjective (superlative of 'bonus')
   best, excellent, very good
   optimal, optimise, optimism,
   optimist, optimistic, optimum

oro

oro, orare, oravi, oratus
verb *(first)*
    beg, beg for
    orate, oration, orator, oratorial,
    oratory

....

....

....

....

ostendo, ostendere, ostendi, ostentus
verb *(third)*
    show
    ostensible, ostensibly, ostensive,
    ostentation, ostentatious

....

....

....

....

P

paene
adverb
   almost, nearly
   *peninsula, peninsular, peninsularity
   (cf. 'insula'), penult, penultimate,
   penumbra*

paro, parare, paravi, paratus
verb *(first)*
   prepare, provide
   *preparation, preparative,
   preparatory, prepare, prepared,
   'semper paratus' (cf. 'semper')*

pars, partis (fem.)
noun (3rd)
   part
   *part, partial, participle, particle,
   parting, partition*

parvus, parva, parvum ....
adjective
    small ....
    parvanimity, parvovirus ....

pater, patris (masc.) ....
noun (3rd)
    father ....
    paternal, paternalism, paternalistic, ...
    paternally, paternity
    (cf. 'frater', 'mater' and 'soror') ....

patior, pati, passus sum*** ....
verb *(third) (deponent)*
    suffer, endure ....
    impassive, passion, passionate, ...
    passive, patience, patient
     ....

patria, patriae (fem.)*** ....
noun (1st)
    country, homeland, fatherland ....
    Patricia, Patrick, patriot, patriotic, ...
    patriotism, repatriate
     ....

pauci, paucae, pauca ....
adjective (pl.)
    few, a few ....
    pauciloquent (cf. 'loquor'), paucity ....

pax, pacis (fem.)
noun (3rd)
    peace
    pacifiable, pacifier, pacifism,
    pacifist, pacify

....
....
....
....

pecunia, pecuniae (fem.)
noun (1st)
    money
    impecunious, pecuniarily,
    pecuniary, pecunious

....
....
....
....

peior, peius
adjective (comparative of 'malus')
    worse
    pejorate, pejoration, pejorative,
    pejoratively
    (cf. note under 'I')

....
....
....
....

pello, pellere, pepuli, pulsus***
verb *(third)*
    drive
    expel, expulsion, impulsive, pulsate,
    pulse, repel

....
....
....
....

per (+ accusative)
(also used as a prefix with verbs)[14*]
preposition
    through, along
    perceive, 'per centum' or 'per cent'
    (cf. 'centum'), percussion, permeate,
    permission, permit (cf. 'mitto'),
    perturb (cf. 'turba')

pereo, perire, perii
verb *(irreg.)*
    die, perish
    perish, perishability, perishable,
    perished, perishing

periculum, periculi (neut.)
noun (2nd)
    danger
    peril, perilous, perilously, perilousness

persuadeo, persuadere, persuasi
(+ dative)
verb *(second)*
    persuade
    persuadable, persuade, persuader,
    persuasion, persuasive,
    persuasiveness

---

[14] The OCR List does not include its use as a prefix with verbs.

perterritus, perterrita, perterritum   ....
adjective
 terrified   ....
 terrified, terrify, terrifying, ...
 terrifyingly, terror, terrorism
 (cf. 'terreo')   ....

pes

THE COLOSSAL **FOOT** OF CONSTANTINE

pes, pedis (masc.)   ....
noun (3rd)
 foot, paw[15]**   ....
 centipede (cf. 'centum'), millipede   ....
 (cf. 'mille'), pedal, pedestrian,
 pedicab, pedicure (cf. 'cura'), ...
 pedometer
       ....

pessimus, pessima, pessimum   ....
adjective (superlative of 'malus')
 worst, very bad   ....
 pessimal, pessimism, pessimist, ...
 pessimistic, pessimum
       ....

---

[15] The second meaning, 'paw', is only given on the Eduqas List and not on the OCR List.

peto, petere, petivi, petitus ....
verb *(third)*
   make for, seek, beg for, ask for, attack ....
   compete, competent, competition, ...
   petition, petitioner, petitioning

....

placeo, placere, placui (+ dative)* ....
verb *(second)*
   please ....
   implacable, placate, placatory, ...
   'placebo', placet

....

plenus, plena, plenum* ....
adjective
   full ....
   replenish, replenished, replenishment

....

plurimus, plurima, plurimum[16] ....
adjective (superlative of 'multus')
   very much, *pl.* very many, most ....
   vide 'plus'

....

---

[16] Although 'plurimus' does not appear as a separate entry on the Eduqas List, learners are expected to be familiar with it as it is the superlative of the adjective 'multus' which is on the Eduqas List. See notes to Appendix One.

The irregular comparatives and superlatives of each of 'bonus' 'malus' 'magnus' and 'parvus' are included on the Eduqas List. Given that 'multus' is currently accompanied only by its comparative 'plus', Eduqas has advised that, for consistency, it intends to amend the Eduqas List to include 'plurimus' at the next syllabus update.

plus, (gen.) pluris
adjective (comparative of 'multus')
    more of (+ gen.); *pl.* more
    plural, pluralism, pluri-, e.g.
    pluripresence (cf. 'sum'), plus

....
....
....
....

poena, poenae (fem.)
noun (1st)
    punishment
    penal, penalisation, penalise,
    penally, penalty

....
....
....
....

pono, ponere, posui, positus
verb *(third)*
    put, place, set up, put up
    deposit, deposition, pose, posit,
    positioning,
    postpone (cf. 'post'),
    preposition, transpose (cf. 'trans')

....
....
....
....
....

porta, portae (fem.)
noun (1st)
    gate
    portal

....
....
....

porto, portare, portavi, portatus
verb *(first)*
    carry, bear, take
    deport, deportation, portability,
    portable, porter, portfolio,
    transport (cf. 'trans')

....
....
....
....

possum, posse, potui[17]**

verb *(irreg.)*

  can, be able

  idempotent (cf. 'idem'), impossible,
  nilpotent (cf. 'nihil'),
  omnipotent (cf. 'omnis'),
  possibility, possible

....
....
....
....
....

post (+ accusative)

preposition

  after, behind

  postdate, postdoctoral, 'post
  meridiem' or 'p.m.' (cf. 'dies'),
  post-mortem (cf. 'mors'),
  postpone (cf. 'pono'),
  'post scriptum' or 'P.S.' (cf. scribo')

....
....
....
....
....
....

postea

adverb

  afterwards

  vide 'post'

....
....
....

postulo, postulare, postulavi, postulatus*

verb *(first)*

  demand

  postulant, postulate, postulation,
  postulatory

....
....
....
....

---

[17] The Eduqas specification does not include the perfect tense of 'sum' or its compounds.

praebo, praebere, praebui, praebitus*
verb *(second)*
   provide
   prebend, prebendal, prebendary

....

....

....

praemium, praemii (neut.)
noun (2nd)
   prize, reward, profit
   premium

....

....

....

primo***
adverb
   at first
   vide 'primus'

....

....

....

primus, prima, primum
adjective
   first
   'prima facie', primary, primate,
   prime, primitive, primordial

....

....

....

....

princeps, principis (masc.)
noun (3rd)
   chief; emperor
   prince, princedom, principal,
   principality, principle

....

....

....

....

pro (+ ablative)
(also used as a prefix with verbs)[18]*
preposition
   in front of, for, in return for
   (as prefix = forwards)
   proactive (cf. 'ago'),
   'pros and cons' (cf. 'contra'),
   proffer (cf. 'offero'),
   pro-forma, 'pro rata',
   'quid pro quo' (cf. 'quis?')

procedo, procedere, processi
verb *(third)*
   advance, proceed
   procedure, proceed, process,
   procession, processionary, processor

proficiscor, proficisci, profectus sum*
verb *(third) (deponent)*
   set out
   profectitious

progredior, progredi, progressus sum
verb *(third) (deponent)*
   advance
   progress (verb and noun),
   progression, progressionary,
   progressionist, progressive

---

[18] The OCR List does not include its use as a prefix with verbs.

promitto, promittere, promisi,
promissus
verb *(third)*
    promise
    promise, promisee, promising,
    promisor, promissive, promissory

....
....
....
....

proximus, proxima, proximum
adjective
    nearest, next to
    approximate, approximation,
    proximal, proximate, proximity

....
....
....
....

puer, pueri (masc.)
noun (2nd)
    boy
    puerile, puerilism, puerility

....
....
....

pugno, pugnare, pugnavi
verb *(first)*
    fight
    pugnacious, pugnaciously,
    pugnaciousness, pugnacity
    (cf. 'oppugno')

....
....
....
....

pulcher, pulchra, pulchrum
adjective
    beautiful, handsome
    pulchritude, pulchritudinous

....
....
....

punio, punire, punivi, punitus***
verb *(fourth)*
 punish
 punish, punishable, punisher,
 punishment, punition, punitive

....

....

....

....

puto, putare, putavi, putatus
verb *(first)*
 think
 putative, putatively

....

....

....

Q

quaero

quaero, quaerere, quaesivi, quaesitus
verb *(third)*
   search for, look for, ask
   enquiry, inquiry, query, quest,
   question, questionnaire

....

....

....

....

qualis?, quale?
adjective
   what sort of?
   quale, qualified, qualify, qualitative,
   quality

....
....
....
....

quantus? quanta? quantum?
adjective
   how big? how much?
   quantifiable, quantify, quantitative,
   quantity, quantum

....
....
....
....

quattuor
number (indecl.)
   four
   quadrangle, quadrilateral,
   quadruple, quarter, quartet,
   quatercentenary (cf. 'centum'),
   quaternary, quaternate

....
....
....
....
....

qui, quae, quod
pronoun
   who, which
   'quod erat demonstrandum' or
   'Q.E.D.', 'quod vide' or 'q.v.',
   quorate, quorum, 'status quo'

....
....
....
....

quinque
number (indecl.)
   five
   quincentenary (cf. 'centum'),
   quinqu(e)-, quinquefoliate,
   quinquennial (cf. 'annus'), quintuplet

quis?, quid?
pronoun
   who?, what?
   'quid pro quo' (cf. 'pro'), quiddity,
   'quidnunc'

quot?
adjective
   how many?
   quota, quotation, quote, quotidian
   (cf. 'dies'), quotient

R

rapio, rapere, rapui, raptus
verb *(third/fourth)*
    seize, grab
    enrapture, rapacious, rapacity, rape,
    rapture

....
....
....
....

re- (a prefix used with verbs)
prefix
    . . . back
    reconvene (cf. 're' and 'convenio'),
    recur (cf. 'curro'),
    re-elect (cf. 'lego'),
    refugee (cf. 'fugio'),
    regain, reinstate, reiterate (cf. 'iterum'),
    renounce, repeat, return

....
....
....
....
....

refero, referre, rettuli, relatus
verb *(irreg.)*
    bring back, carry back; report, tell
    refer, referee, referral, relate, related,
    relation, relative

....
....
....

regina, reginae (fem.) ....

noun (1st)

    queen ....

    regal, regally, regency, regent, ...
    Regina/Gina, regius
    (cf. 'regnum', 'rego' and 'rex') ....

regnum, regni (neut.)*** ....

noun (2nd)

    kingdom ....

    regal, regalian, regality, regency, ...
    regnal, regnant
    (cf. 'regina', 'rego' and 'rex') ....

rego, regere, rexi, rectus*** ....

verb *(third)*

    rule, reign ....

    regent, regentship, regiment, ...
    regimental, regular, regulate
    (cf. 'regina', 'regnum' and 'rex') ....

regredior, regredi, regressus sum ....

verb *(third/fourth) (deponent)*

    go back, return ....

    regress, regression, regressive, ...
    regressivity

     ....

relinquo, relinquere, reliqui, relictus ....

verb *(third)*

    leave, leave behind ....

    relic, relict, relinquish, relinquished, ...
    relinquishment, reliquary

     ....

res, rei (fem.)
noun (5th)
    thing, matter, event, business
    're'

....

....

....

resisto, resistere, restiti (+ dative)
verb *(third)*
    resist
    irresistible, resist, resistance,
    resistible, resistivity,
    resistor

....

....

....

....

respondeo, respondere, respondi,
responsus
verb *(second)*
    reply
    irresponsible, respond, responder,
    response, responsible, responsive

....

....

....

....

rex, regis (masc.)
noun (3rd)
    king
    regalia, regalist, regally, regius, Rex
    (cf. 'regina', 'regnum' and 'rego')

....

....

....

....

rideo

rideo, ridere, risi ....
verb *(second)* ....
   laugh, smile ....
   deride, derision, derisory, rident,
   ridicule, ridiculous

....

rogo, rogare, rogavi, rogatus ....
verb *(first)* ....
   ask, ask for
   rogation, rogatory ....

....

S

sacer, sacra, sacrum
adjective
    sacred
    sacrament, sacred, sacrifice,
    sacrificial, sacrilege

....

....

....

....

saluto, salutare, salutavi, salutatus
verb *(first)*
    greet
    salutary, salutation, salutational,
    salute, saluter

....

....

....

....

sanguis, sanguinis (masc.)
noun (3rd)
    blood
    sanguiferous, sanguify, sanguine,
    sanguinely, sanguivorous

....

....

....

....

scelestus, scelesta, scelestum***
adjective
   wicked
   scelerate
   (cf. 'scelus')

....

....

....

....

scelus, sceleris (neut.)***
noun (3rd)
   crime
   scelerate
   (cf. 'scelestus')

....

....

....

....

scio, scire, scivi, scitus
verb *(fourth)*
   know
   nescient (cf. 'nescio'), omniscient
   (cf. 'omnis'), science, scient, scientific,
   scientist

....

....

....

....

scribo, scribere, scripsi, scriptus
verb *(third)*
   write
   manuscript (cf. 'manus'), 'post
   scriptum' or 'P.S.' (cf. 'post'), scribble,
   scribe, script, scripture

....

....

....

....

sedeo, sedere, sedi
verb *(second)*
   sit
   sedent, sedentarily, sedentariness,
   sedentary

....

....

....

....

semper
adverb
  always
  *'semper fidelis' (cf. 'fidelis'), 'semper
  idem' (cf. 'idem'),
  'semper paratus' (cf. 'paro'),
  sempervivum (cf. 'vivo'),
  sempiternal*

....

....

....

....

....

senator, senatoris (masc.)
noun (3rd)
  senator
  *senate, senate-house, senator,
  senatorial, senatorship*

....

....

....

....

senex, senis (masc.)
noun (3rd)
  old man
  *senile, senilely, senility, senior,
  seniority*

....

....

....

....

sentio, sentire, sensi, sensus
verb *(fourth)*
  feel, notice
  *sense, senseless, sensory, sensual,
  sentence, sentiment*

....

....

....

....

septem
number (indecl.)
    seven
    September, septennial (cf. annus),
    septuplet

....

....

....

....

sequor, sequi, secutus sum
verb *(third) (deponent)*
    follow
    consequence, second, sequacious,
    sequel, sequence, sequential

....

....

....

....

servo, servare, servavi, servatus
verb *(first)*
    save, keep, protect
    conservation, conservatory, conserve,
    observe, preserve, reserve

....

....

....

....

servus, servi (masc.)
noun *(second)*
    slave[19]
    servile, servility, servitude

....

....

....

sex
number (indecl.)
    six
    sex-, sexcentenary, sexennial
    (cf. annus), sexpartite, sextuplet

....

....

....

....

---

[19] Avoid translating 'servus' as servant.

sic
adverb
   thus, in this way
   'sic', 'sic passim'

signum, signi (neut.)*
noun (2nd)
   sign, signal, seal
   signage, signalise, signalling,
   signature, signet, signify

silva

silva, silvae (fem.)
noun (1st)
   wood
   silva, silvan, silvatic, silvestrian,
   Silvia, silviculture

simul****
adverb
    at the same time
    simultaneity, simultaneous,
    simultaneously, simultaneousness

....
....
....
....

sine (+ ablative)
preposition
    without
    sinecure (cf. 'cura'), 'sine die',
    'sine dubio', 'sine qua non'

....
....
....
....

soleo, solere, solitus sum****
verb *(second) (semi-deponent)*
    be accustomed
    insolence, insolent, obsolescence,
    obsolescent, obsolete

....
....
....
....

solus, sola, solum
adjective
    alone, lonely, only, on one's own
    solitary, solitude, solitudinarian,
    solivagant, solo

....
....
....
....

soror, sororis (fem.)[20]   ....

noun (3rd)   ....
   sister
   sororal, sororial, sororicide, ...
   sororise, sorority
   (cf. 'frater', 'mater' and 'pater')   ....

specto, spectare, spectavi, spectatus   ....

verb *(first)*
   look at, watch   ....
   spectacle, spectacled, spectacular, ...
   spectate, spectator, spectatorship

   ....

spero, sperare, speravi, speratus***   ....

verb *(first)*
   hope, expect   ....
   despair, desperate, desperation   ....
   (cf. 'despero' and 'spes')

   ....

spes, spei (fem.)   ....

noun *(fifth)*
   hope   ....
   despair, desperate, desperation   ....
   (cf. 'despero' and 'spero')

   ....

---

[20] The OCR List does not include 'soror' although it does include 'frater', 'mater' and 'pater'.

sto, stare, steti
verb *(first)*
    stand
    stance, standing, station, stationary,
    stationery, 'stet'

....

....

....

....

stultus, stulta, stultum
adjective
    stupid, foolish
    stultification, stultified, stultifier,
    stultify, stultifying

....

....

....

....

sub (+ accusative/ablative)
(also used as a prefix with verbs)[21]*
preposition
    under, beneath
    (as prefix = under, up to)
    submarine (cf. 'mare'), submerge,
    subordinate, subsidiary,
    substandard, suburban (cf. 'urbs'),
    subway

....

....

....

....

....

....

subito
adverb
    suddenly
    subitaneous, subitise

....

....

....

---

[21] The OCR List does not include its use as a prefix with verbs.

sum, esse, fui[22]**   ....
verb *(irreg.)*   ....
    be   ....
    essence, essential, essentialism,
    'id est' or 'i.e.', presence, present   ....

    ....

summus, summa, summum   ....
adjective
    highest, greatest, top (of)   ....
    sum, 'summa cum laude'
    (cf. 'cum' and 'laudo'), ...
    summit, summitless   ....

supero, superare, superavi, superatus   ....
verb *(first)*
    overcome, overpower   ....
    insuperable, superable, superably,
    superate, superation   ....

    ....

surgo, surgere, surrexi   ....
verb *(third)*
    get up, stand up, rise   ....
    resurge, resurgence, surge, surgeful,
    surgent, surging   ....

    ....

---

[22] The Eduqas specification does not include the perfect tense of 'sum' or its compounds.

T

taberna, tabernae (fem.)
noun (1st)
    shop, inn
    tabernacle, tabernacular, tavern,
    taverna, taverner

....

....

....

....

taceo, tacere, tacui, tacitus
verb *(second)*
    be silent, be quiet, keep quiet
    tacit, tacitly, tacitness, taciturn,
    taciturnity, taciturnly

....

....

....

....

talis, tale
adjective
    such, of such a kind
    talesman
    (N.B. different from talisman)

....

....

....

....

tandem

tandem
adverb
  at last, finally
  (in) tandem, tandem

tempestas, tempestatis (fem.)***
noun (3rd)
  storm
  tempest, tempestive, tempestuous,
  tempestuously, tempestuousness

templum, templi (neut.)
noun (2nd)
  temple
  templar, temple, templed

tempus, temporis (neut.) ....

noun (3rd) ....

    time ....

    contemporaneous, contemporary, ...
    'pro tempore' or 'pro tem.' (cf. 'pro'),
    temporal, temporary, temporise, tense ....

teneo, tenere, tenui, tentus ....

verb *(second)*

    hold, keep ....

    abstain (cf. 'ab'), tenable, tenacious, ...
    tenacity, tenancy, tenure

....

terra, terrae (fem.) ....

noun (1st)

    ground, land, country, earth ....

    extraterrestrial, Mediterranean ....
    (cf. 'medius'), 'terra firma', terrace,
    terracing, terrene, terrestrial ....

terreo, terrere, terrui, territus ....

verb *(second)*

    frighten ....

    terrified, terrify, terrifying, ...
    terrifyingly, terror, terrorism
    (cf. 'perterritus') ....

timeo, timere, timui ....

verb *(second)*

    fear, be afraid ....

    timid, timidity, timidly, timidness, ...
    timorous

....

tollo, tollere, sustuli, sublatus
verb *(third)*
    raise, lift up, hold up
    sublate, sublation

....

....

....

....

tot
adjective
    so many
    tot (up) (cf. 'totus')

....

....

....

....

totus, tota, totum
adjective
    whole
    total, totalise, totalitarian, totality,
    totally

....

....

....

....

trado, tradere, tradidi, traditus
verb *(third)*
    hand over, hand down
    tradition, traditional, traditionalist,
    traditionalistic, traditionally

....

....

....

....

traho, trahere, traxi, tractus
verb *(third)*
    drag
    protractor, retract, retractable, tract,
    tractable, traction, tractor

....

....

....

....

trans (+ accusative)
(also used as a prefix with verbs)
preposition
    across
    transatlantic, transcend, transfer
    (cf. 'fero'), translation, translucent
    (cf. 'lux'), transport (cf. 'porto'),
    transpose (cf. 'pono'), transvestite

tres, tria
number
    three
    tri-, triad, triangle, triathlon,
    triceps (cf. 'caput')

tristis, triste
adjective
    sad
    triste, tristesse

turba, turbae (fem.)
noun (1st)
    crowd
    perturb, perturbance (cf. 'per'),
    turbid, turbulator, turbulence,
    turbulent

tutus, tuta, tutum*
adjective
    safe
    tutee, tutor, tutorage, tutorial,
    tutorship

U

ubi
adverb
    where, when, with '?' = where?
    ubiety, ubiquarian, ubiquitary,
    ubiquitous, ubiquity

....
....
....
....

unus, una, unum
number
    one
    uni-, unicorn, uniform, unify,
    unitard, unity,
    universe (cf. 'verto'),
    university

....
....
....
....
....

urbs, urbis (fem.)
noun (3rd)
    city, town
    suburban (cf. 'sub'), urban, urbane,
    urbanism, urbanite

....
....
....
....

uxor

uxor, uxoris (fem.)   ....
noun (3rd)
    wife   ....
    uxorial, uxorially, uxorilocal   ....
    (cf. 'locus'), uxorious

                                              ....

V

validus, valida, validum***
adjective
   strong
   invalid, invalidate, valid, validate,
   validation, validity

....

....

....

....

vehementer
adverb
   violently, loudly, strongly
   vehemence, vehemency, vehement,
   vehemently

....

....

....

....

vendo, vendere, vendidi, venditus
verb *(third)*
   sell
   vend, vendibility, vendible, vending,
   vendition, vendor

....

....

....

....

venio, venire, veni

....

verb *(fourth)*

....

    come

....

    advent (cf. 'advenio'), circumvent
    (cf. 'circum'),

....

    contravene (cf. 'contra'),

....

    convenient, convent, convention,
    reconvene (cf. 're' and 'convenio')

....

verbum, verbi (neut.)

....

noun (2nd)

....

    word

....

    adverb (cf. 'ad'), cruciverbalist,
    verb, verbal, verbality,

....

    verbatim, verbose

....

....

verto, vertere, verti, versus***

....

verb *(third)*

....

    turn

....

    convert, divert, reverse (cf. 're'),
    verse, version, vertebra,

....

    'vice versa'

....

verus, vera, verum*

....

adjective

....

    true, real

....

    verification, verify, verisimilitude,
    verism, veritable, Verity

....

....

vestimenta, vestimentorum (neut. pl.)* ....
noun (2nd)
   clothes ....
   divest, invest, investiture, investment, ...
   vest, vested
....

via, viae (fem.) ....
noun (1st)
   street, road, way ....
   via, viaduct (cf. 'duco')
....

victoria, victoriae (fem.)*** ....
noun (1st)
   victory ....
   Victor, victor, Victoria, victorious, ...
   victoriousness, victory
   (cf. 'vinco') ....

video, videre, vidi, visus ....
verb *(second)*
   see ....
   audio-visual (cf. 'audio'), video, visa, ...
   visibility, vision, vista, visual
....

villa, villae (fem.) ....
noun (1st)
   house, country villa ....
   villa, village ....

vinco, vincere, vici, victus
....
verb *(third)*
....
   conquer, win, be victorious
   vanquish, vanquishable, vanquisher,
....
   Vincent
   (cf. 'victoria')
....

vinum

vinum, vini (neut.)
....
noun (2nd)
   wine
....
   vine, vinegar, vineyard, viniculture,
....
   vintage, vintner
....

vir, viri (masc.)
....
noun (2nd)
   man, male
....
   virago, virile, virilescence, virility,
....
   virtue
   (cf. 'virtus')
....

virtus, virtutis (fem.)***   ....

noun (3rd)

   courage, virtue   ....

   virtual, virtue, virtuosity, virtuous, ...
   virtuously

   (cf. 'vir')   ....

vita, vitae (fem.)   ....

noun (1st)

   life   ....

   'curriculum vitae' or 'C.V.', Vita, ...
   vital, vitality, vitamin

   ....

vivo, vivere, vixi   ....

verb *(third)*

   live, be alive   ....

   sempervivum (cf. 'semper'), ...
   vivacious, vivacity,

   'viva voce' or 'viva' (cf. 'vox'), ...
   Vivian, vivid, vividness, vivisection

   (cf. 'vivus')   ....

   ....

vivus, viva, vivum*   ....

adjective

   alive, living   ....

   vivacious, vivarium, viviparous, ...
   vivisect, vivisection

   (cf. 'vivo')   ....

voco, vocare, vocavi, vocatus ....
verb *(first)* ....
    call ....
    vocabulary, vocal, vocalise, vocation,
    vocative ....
    (cf. 'vox') ....

volo, velle, volui ....
verb *(irreg.)* ....
    want, wish, be willing ....
    benevolent (cf. 'bene'),
    volition, volitive, voluntarily, ...
    voluntary, volunteer
    (cf. 'nolo') ....
    ....

vox, vocis (fem.) ....
noun (3rd)
    voice, shout ....
    'viva voce' or 'viva' (cf. 'vivo'),
    vocal, vocals, vocative, vociferate, ...
    vociferous
    (cf. 'voco') ....
    ....

vulnero, vulnerare, vulneravi, ...
vulneratus***
verb *(first)* ....
    wound, injure ....
    invulnerable, vulnerability,
    vulnerable, vulnerary, vulnerate, ...
    vulneration
    (cf. 'vulnus') ....

vulnus, vulneris (neut.)   ....
noun (3rd)
   wound   ....
   invulnerable, vulnerability,
   vulnerable, vulnerary, vulnerate, ...
   vulneration   ....
   (cf. 'vulnero')
                                  ....

Appendix One: Additional words in the Eduqas Defined Vocabulary List

Together with the words indicated in the main entries, this appendix forms the Defined Vocabulary List ('the Eduqas List') which is required for Component 1 (Section A). There are 440 entries in the Eduqas List.

Learners are expected to be familiar with all the words in the Eduqas List. Words used in the Momentum Test (Section A of the paper) will be glossed if they do not appear in the Eduqas List. In addition, if a word is used with a meaning not given in the Eduqas List, it will be glossed.

For Section B, in the grammar question, all the words will be taken from the Eduqas List.

In addition to the words in the Eduqas List, learners are expected to be familiar with the following forms:

Compound verbs

Learners are expected to be familiar with common compounds of simple verbs given in the Eduqas List which are formed by adding one of the prefixes included in the Eduqas List, and where the basic meanings of the prefix and stem are retained. This includes regular vowel changes in the verb stem and consonantal changes in the prefix.

Adjectives

Learners are expected to be familiar with the comparative and superlative forms of all adjectives included in the Eduqas List.

Adverbs

Learners are expected to be familiar with the regular formation of adverbs from any of the adjectives which appear in the Eduqas List, including regular superlative forms.

Numbers

Those included in the Eduqas List are expected to be known (these are included in the main entries of this Lexicon). All others will be glossed on the examination paper.

ac, atque	*indecl.*	*conjunction*	and
adeo	*indecl.*	*adverb*	so much, so greatly
aliquis*	aliquid	*pronoun*	someone, something
apud*	*+ accusative*	*preposition*	among, with, at the house of
aut ... aut*	*indecl.*	*conjunction*	either ... or
coepi	coepisse, coeptus	*verb (perfect tense)*	began
cum	*indecl.*	*conjunction*	when, since
cur?	*indecl.*	*adverb*	why?
deinde	*indecl.*	*adverb*	then
dives*	*gen.* divitis	*adjective*	rich
dum	*indecl.*	*conjunction*	while
enim	*indecl.*	*conjunction*	for
et	*indecl.*	*conjunction*	and
etiam	*indecl.*	*adverb*	also, even
habeo	habere, habui, habitus	*verb (second)*	have

heri	*indecl.*	*adverb*	yesterday
hic*	*indecl.*	*adverb*	here
hic	haec, hoc	*pronoun*	this
iam	*indecl.*	*adverb*	now, already
igitur	*indecl.*	*adverb*	therefore, and so
ille	illa, illud	*pronoun*	that, he, she, it
ingens	*gen.* ingentis	*adjective*	huge
inquit		*verb (irreg.)*	he/she says, he/she said
ita	*indecl.*	*adverb*	in this way, so
ita vero*	*indecl.*	*adverb*	yes
itaque	*indecl.*	*adverb*	and so, therefore
libenter	*indecl.*	*adverb*	willingly, gladly
liberi	liberorum *masc. pl.*	*noun (2nd)*	children
magnopere*	*indecl.*	*adverb*	greatly, very much
mox	*indecl.*	*adverb*	soon
nam	*indecl.*	*conjunction*	for
ne	*indecl.*	*conjunction*	that . . . not, so that . . . not
-ne . . .? (added to end of a word)	*indecl.*	*particle*	(introduces question)

nec . . . nec, neque . . . neque	*indecl.*	*conjunction*	neither . . . nor
neco	necare, necavi, necatus	*verb (first)*	kill
nemo[1]	neminis	*noun (irreg.)*	no one, nobody
nonne . . . ?	*indecl.*	*adverb*	surely?
noster	nostra, nostrum	*pronoun*	our
num	*indecl.*	*particle*	whether
num . . . ?	*indecl.*	*particle*	surely . . . not?
numquam	*indecl.*	*adverb*	never
nunc	*indecl.*	*adverb*	now
occido	occidere, occidi, occisus	*verb (third)*	kill
olim	*indecl.*	*adverb*	once, some time ago
pareo*	parere, parui + *dative*	*verb (second)*	obey
poenas do (*vide* main entry for poena)	dare, dedi, datus		pay the penalty, be punished
postquam	*indecl.*	*conjunction*	after, when

---

[1] The genitive of 'nemo' is given as 'neminis'. Eduqas has confirmed that this is for historical reasons and that when it updates the Eduqas List, 'neminis' will be replaced with 'nullius'. The OCR List uses 'nullius' and this is the norm in classical Latin prose. (Thank you to John Taylor for the latter point.)

postridie	*indecl.*	*adverb*	on the next day
prope	+ *accusative*	*preposition*	near
propter	+ *accusative*	*preposition*	because of
puella	puellae *fem.*	*noun (1st)*	girl
quam	*indecl.*	*adverb*	than, how ...? how ...!
quamquam	*indecl.*	*conjunction*	although
-que (added to end of a word)	*indecl.*	*conjunction*	and
quo?	*indecl.*	*adverb*	where to?
quod	*indecl.*	*conjunction*	because
quo modo?[2]	*indecl.*	*adverb*	how? in what way?
quoque	*indecl.*	*conjunction*	also, too
reddo	reddere, reddidi, redditus	*verb (third)*	give back, restore
redeo	redire, redii	*verb (irreg.)*	go back, come back, return
Roma	Romae *fem.* (Romae: at/in Rome)	*noun (1st)*	Rome

[2] 'quo modo' is shown as two words. An alternative is 'quomodo' as one word and this is the form which is on the OCR List.

Romanus	Romana, Romanum	*adjective*	Roman
saepe	*indecl.*	*adverb*	often
saevus	saeva, saevum	*adjective*	savage, cruel
se	sui	*reflexive pronoun*	himself, herself, itself, themselves
sed	*indecl.*	*conjunction*	but
si	*indecl.*	*conjunction*	if
sicut*	*indecl.*	*adverb*	just as, like
simulac, simulatque	*indecl.*	*conjunction*	as soon as
statim	*indecl.*	*adverb*	at once, immediately
suus	sua, suum	*pronoun*	his, her, its, their (own)
tam	*indecl.*	*adverb*	so
tamen	*indecl.*	*adverb*	however
tantus	tanta, tantum	*adjective*	so great, such a great, so much
tu	tui	*pronoun*	you (singular)
tum	*indecl.*	*adverb*	then
tuus	tua, tuum	*pronoun*	your (singular), yours
umquam	*indecl.*	*adverb*	ever

unde	*indecl.*	*adverb*	from where
ut	*indecl.* + subjunctive	*conjunction*	that, so that, in order that
ut	*indecl.* + indicative	*conjunction*	as
vester	vestra, vestrum	*pronoun*	your (plural), yours
vix*	*indecl.*	*adverb*	scarcely, hardly, with difficulty
vos	vestrum	*pronoun*	you (plural)
vultus*	vultus *masc.*	*noun (4th)*	expression, face

Appendix Two: Additional words in the OCR Defined Vocabulary List

Together with the words indicated in the main entries, this appendix forms the Defined Vocabulary List ('the OCR List') which is required for the Latin-English sections of Latin GCSE (9-1), Component 01, *Language*. There are 450 entries in the OCR List.

In addition to the words in the OCR List, candidates are expected to be familiar with the following forms:

- all regular adverbs formed from the listed adjectives;
- comparative and superlative forms of all listed adjectives and corresponding adverbs (for ease of reference, the

irregular comparative and superlative forms of 'bonus', 'malus', 'magnus', 'parvus' and 'multus' are included in the main entries of this Lexicon);

- cardinal numbers 1 to 10, 100, 1000 (these are included in the main entries of this Lexicon);

- compound verbs which are formed by using the prefixes contained in the list (e.g. 'remitto', I send back).

All other words in a passage will be glossed. When a word from the OCR List appears in a passage with a meaning that is not given in the OCR List, it will be glossed.

ac, atque	*indecl.*	*conjunction*	and
adeo	*indecl.*	*adverb*	so much, so greatly, to such an extent
alii ... alii***			some ... others
coepi[1]	coepisse	*verb irreg.*	began
cum	*indecl.*	*conjunction*	when, since
cur?	*indecl.*	*adverb*	why?
deinde	*indecl.*	*adverb*	then
dum	*indecl.*	*conjunction*	while, until

---

[1] The verb 'coepi' is given with its infinitive 'coepisse' but the perfect passive participle 'coeptus' is not included. cf. the Eduqas List which includes all three forms.

ecce!***	*indecl.*	*adverb*	look!
enim	*indecl.*	*conjunction*	for
et	*indecl.*	*conjunction*	and, even
et ... et***	*indecl.*		both ... and
etiam	*indecl.*	*adverb*	also, even
habeo	habere, habui, habitus	*verb (second)*	have, hold
heri	*indecl.*	*adverb*	yesterday
hic	haec, hoc	*pronoun*	this; he, she, it
iam	*indecl.*	*adverb*	now, already
igitur	*indecl.*	*adverb*	therefore, and so
ille	illa, illud	*pronoun*	that; he, she, it
ingens	*gen.* ingentis	*adjective*	huge
inquit		*verb (irreg.)*	he/she says, he/she said
interficio***	interficere, interfeci, interfectus	*verb (third/fourth)*	kill
ita	*indecl.*	*adverb*	in this way, to such an extent, so
itaque	*indecl.*	*adverb*	and so, therefore
libenter	*indecl.*	*adverb*	willingly, gladly

liberi	liberorum *masc. pl.*	*noun (2nd)*	children
malo***	malle, malui	*verb (irreg.)*	prefer
mox	*indecl.*	*adverb*	soon
nam	*indecl.*	*conjunction*	for
-ne ...?	*indecl.*	*particle*	(introduces question)
ne	*indecl.* + subjunctive	*conjunction*	that ... not, so that ... not; (after verb of fearing) that, lest
nec, neque	*indecl.*	*conjunction*	and not, nor, neither
neco	necare, necavi, necatus	*verb (first)*	kill
nemo[2]	nullius	*noun (irreg.)*	no one, nobody
nisi***	*indecl.*	*conjunction*	unless, except
nonne ...?	*indecl.*	*adverb*	surely ...?
nonnulli***	nonnullae, nonnulla	*adjective*	some, several
noster	nostra, nostrum	*pronoun*	our
num	*indecl.*	*particle*	whether

[2] The genitive of 'nemo' is given as 'nullius': cf. the corresponding entry and footnote on the Eduqas List. 'nullius' is the norm in classical Latin prose. (Thank you to John Taylor for the latter point.)

num ...?	*indecl.*	*particle*	surely ... not?
numquam	*indecl.*	*adverb*	never
nunc	*indecl.*	*adverb*	now
occido	occidere, occidi, occisus	*verb (third)*	kill
olim	*indecl.*	*adverb*	once, some time ago
poenas do (*vide* main entry for poena)	dare, dedi, datus		pay the penalty, be punished
postquam	*indecl.*	*conjunction*	after, when
postridie	*indecl.*	*adverb*	on the next day
proelium***	proelii *neut.*	*noun (2nd)*	battle
prope	+ accusative	*preposition*	near
propter	+ accusative	*preposition*	on account of, because of
puella	puellae *fem.*	*noun (1st)*	girl
quam***	+ superlative adverb		as ... as possible
quam	*indecl.*	*adverb*	than; how ...? how ...!
quamquam	*indecl.*	*conjunction*	although
quando?***	*indecl.*	*adverb*	when?
-que	*indecl.*	*conjunction*	and

quidam***	quaedam, quoddam	*pronoun*	one, a certain, some
quo?	*indecl.*	*adverb*	to where?
quod	*indecl.*	*conjunction*	because
quomodo?[3]	*indecl.*	*adverb*	how?
quoque	*indecl.*	*conjunction*	also, too
reddo	reddere, reddidi, redditus	*verb (third)*	give back, restore
redeo	redire, redii	*verb (irreg.)*	go back, come back, return
Roma	Romae *fem.* (Romae: at/in Rome)	*noun (1st)*	Rome
Romanus	Romana, Romanum	*adjective*	Roman
saepe	*indecl.*	*adverb*	often
saevus	saeva, saevum	*adjective*	savage, cruel
se	sui	*reflexive pronoun*	himself, herself, itself, themselves
sed	*indecl.*	*conjunction*	but
si	*indecl.*	*conjunction*	if
simulac, simulatque	*indecl.*	*conjunction*	as soon as

[3] 'quomodo' is shown as one word. An alternative is 'quo modo' as two words and this is the form which is on the Eduqas List.

statim	*indecl.*	*adverb*	at once, immediately
suus	sua, suum	*pronoun*	his, her, its, their (own)
tam	*indecl.*	*adverb*	so
tamen	*indecl.*	*adverb*	however
tantus	tanta, tantum	*adjective*	so great, such a great
tu	tui	*pronoun*	you (singular)
tum	*indecl.*	*adverb*	then
tuus	tua, tuum	*pronoun*	your (singular), yours
umquam	*indecl.*	*adverb*	ever
unde?	*indecl.*	*adverb*	from where?
ut	*indecl.* + subjunctive	*conjunction*	that, so that, in order that
ut	*indecl.* + indicative	*conjunction*	as, when
vester	vestra, vestrum	*pronoun*	your (plural), yours
videor***	videri, visus sum	*verb (second) deponent*	seem, appear
vos	vestrum	*pronoun*	you (plural)

Printed in the USA
CPSIA information can be obtained
at www.ICGtesting.com
LVHW020840171024
794056LV00002B/311